# A Short Guide to Writing about Law

# A Short Guide to Writing about Law

## KATIE ROSE GUEST PRYAL
*University of North Carolina at Chapel Hill*

**Longman**
Boston   Columbus   Indianapolis   New York   San Francisco
Upper Saddle River   Amsterdam   Cape Town   Dubai   London   Madrid
Milan   Munich   Paris   Montreal   Toronto   Delhi   Mexico City   Sao Paulo
Sydney   Hong Kong   Seoul   Singapore   Taipei   Tokyo

**Senior Sponsoring Editor:** Virginia L. Blanford
**Executive Marketing Manager:** Megan Galvin Fak
**Project Coordination, Text Design,**
**and Electronic Page Makeup:** Rakesh Poddar, Aptara®, Inc.
**Creative Art Director:** Jayne Conte
**Cover Designer:** Suzanne Behnke
**Cover Illustration/Photo:** Fotolia: Justice © Photosani
**Project Manager:** Renata Butera
**Operations Specialist:** Renata Butera
**Printer/Binder:** Edwards Brothers
**Cover Printer:** Lehigh-Phoenix/Hagerstown

---

**Library of Congress Cataloging-in-Publication Data**

Pryal, Katie Rose Guest.
  A short guide to writing about law / Katie Rose Guest Pryal.
    p. cm.
  ISBN-13: 978-0-205-75201-0
  ISBN-10: 0-205-75201-2
  1. Legal composition.    2. Academic writing.    I. Title.
  KF250.P79 2010
  808′.06634—dc22

                                        2010014582

                    1  2  3  4  5  6  7  8  9  10— EB —13  12  11  10

**Longman**
is an imprint of

ISBN-10:       0-205-75201-2
**www.pearsonhighered.com**  ISBN-13: 978-0-205-75201-0

# Brief Contents

# Contents

# Preface

This book fills a gap: It teaches nonlawyers and nonlaw students how to write about law. Law is a complex professional discourse that has begun to creep into undergraduate courses in a variety of disciplines, including not only prelaw, but also political science, criminal justice, sociology, and interdisciplinary fields such as law and literature. Here, students will find an accessible introduction to the rhetoric of law, legal opinions, and statutes, as well as to wide-access online search engines for conducting legal research. The book includes guidance for producing a variety of pre-professional and scholarly legal genres, including research papers, as well as ways to share this research with the wider community via conference presentations and scholarly publishing.

The most challenging aspect of writing about law is understanding legal discourse. Legal discourse employs a highly specialized vocabulary and a variety of rhetorical devices within a range of obscure genres and document forms. This book addresses each of these challenges.

- *Vocabulary.* Because judges and lawyers write in a highly specialized language with vocabulary that spans a thousand years and a variety of languages, key legal terms appear in this text in bold. They are defined in the text, as well as in a glossary in an appendix.
- *Legal genres.* This book takes a genre-based approach to legal discourse. It addresses some genres as *writing projects* (such as the case brief and the scholarly research paper) and some as *sources of legal authority* (such as the judicial opinion or appellate brief). Whenever a legal genre arises in the text for the first time, the book defines its purpose and describes its uses in legal practice.
- *Rhetorical devices.* The first lawyers were rhetoricians, and the first rhetoricians were lawyers; the study of law through the lens of rhetoric is therefore not only an obvious choice, but it is also an essential one. Rhetoric and composition theories guide this book.

In the end, this is a book about writing well: about inventing sound arguments, conducting thorough research, and using that research to support arguments in a well-organized and eloquent final document. These are the tools of legal writing in particular, but also of academic writing in general. The many interactions between legal writing and academic writing anchor this book. Legal writing emphasizes strength of research and authority, deep attention to organization, and a persuasive tone that manages to be purpose driven and maintain critical distance simultaneously.

This is a short book, necessarily narrow in scope. Most of the cases examined here were decided by the U.S. Supreme Court and address constitutional questions of equal protection and due process. The book is intended to be used, however, with any sequence of cases from any area of law. In fact, this book provides great flexibility to instructors. It will work well as a reference for any course in which students read or write legal discourse, such as political science courses or history courses.

The book focuses on Modern Language Association (MLA) and American Psychological Association (APA) citation styles. Chapter 6 draws on the modest coverage of legal documents in MLA and APA styles and combines this coverage with principles of a professional legal citation style, called Bluebook, to create useful citation guidelines for nonlawyers. The book also provides guidance on general principles of citation and encourages students to recognize that many citation styles share these principles.

Lastly, this book focuses on the genres that support academic writing about law, such as the research paper, the student case brief, and the argument-based outline. It does not focus on the genres of professional legal writing that are typically taught in a law school first-year writing course —the office memo, the appellate brief, the demand letter, and other documents. Chapter 1 discusses the differences and similarities of academic legal writing and professional legal writing. This book covers the former rather than the latter for two reasons: because there are few resources for students who want to incorporate legal texts into their academic writing, and because there are many excellent textbooks on writing professional legal genres.

## OVERVIEW OF CHAPTERS

- Chapter 1 first offers a brief overview of the U.S. legal system and the key terms that students who write about law in academic papers must understand. The main part of Chapter 1, however, focuses on the principles of rhetorical and legal reasoning, reaching back to the Sophists of ancient Greece. This chapter reviews the rhetorical triangle, which most students will have encountered in their first-year writing courses, and culminates with guidelines for writing a rhetorical analysis of a court opinion.

- Chapter 2 introduces court opinions and the appellate process generally. Readers learn the genre of the case brief and the use of legal *topoi* to analyze judicial rhetoric.
- Chapter 3 introduces the genre of scholarly legal writing, including guidance in framing legal arguments, developing a topic for research, and writing an argument-based outline.
- Chapter 4 provides a primer on legal research for nonlawyers, that is, for those who do not have access to expensive professional legal research databases. This chapter provides an annotated list of open-access databases, as well as databases commonly subscribed to by university libraries.
- Chapter 5 draws from the strong organizational frameworks of professional legal genres to guide scholarly writers in shaping effective research papers. The chapter focuses on writing a variety of effective and eloquent paragraphs.
- Chapter 6 introduces principles of citation in academic writing generally and in legal writing in particular. This chapter also discusses ways to integrate legal sources into scholarly writing and cite them properly.
- Chapter 7 provides detailed guidance for revision of scholarly writing. This chapter gives tips for both solo revision and peer workshop revision, and it details common errors made by writers new to legal discourse.
- Chapter 8 provides guidance for oral presentations, including conference presentations of scholarly research. The chapter also walks readers through the steps of publication in scholarly journals, including undergraduate journals.

# Acknowledgments

I would like to thank Jack Boger, Ruth McKinney, and the late John O. Calmore of the University of North Carolina School of Law, who taught me how to research and write about law; Judge Terrence Boyle of the U.S. District Court of the Eastern District of North Carolina, who taught me how law works; and Hephzibah Roskelly of the University of North Carolina at Greensboro, who taught me about rhetoric.

I am gratefull to the following reviewers, who provided helpful suggestions during the writing of this book: Susan Borland, University of Illinois; Gina Genova, University of California/Santa Barbara; Jared Haynes, University of California, Davis Jordynn Jack, University of North Carolina; Nancy Koerbel, University of Pittsburgh; Aaron R.S. Lorenz, Ramapo College; Richard Poland, Flagler College; and Austin Sarat, Amherst College.

My Writing in Law students at the University of North Carolina at Chapel Hill were invaluable contributors to this book, as their questions are the ones I try to answer here. Jordynn Jack and Jane Danielewicz of the UNC Writing Program supported me in designing and teaching Writing in Law. Tonya Hassell, of the Appalachian State University Writing Center, read every chapter of this book closely. Michael Pryal brewed the coffee and changed the diapers so I could write.

Katie Rose Guest Pryal

# A Short Guide to Writing about Law

# 1

# WRITING ABOUT LAW

## WHY WRITE ABOUT LAW?

*Legal writing* is a phrase with several meanings:

- It can refer to *the documents that lawyers produce in practice*, such as client letters, office memos, and appellate briefs. These are the professional documents of lawyers.
- It can refer to *the court opinions drafted by judges* and *statutes drafted by legislators*. These are the documents that compose law.
- It can refer to *academic legal writing*, or *legal scholarship*. Legal scholarship is published in law journals and law reviews and is written by lawyers, judges, law students, and law professors.

The documents within each of these legal **genres** are designed to accomplish certain purposes and therefore share certain sets of conventions. These conventions help lawyers identify a certain type of document as an office memo (because it is addressed to a lawyer in a firm and written in an objective tone) or a brief for a judge (because it is addressed to a judge and written in a persuasive tone).

All of these legal genres share two important characteristics. All make legal claims or observations, and all use primary and secondary legal sources to support these claims. Even a letter written by a lawyer to advise a client makes a legal claim—for example, the likelihood of the client's success in court—and gives reasons for that claim. **Legal writing**, then, can be thought of as *the skill of making legal claims and supporting them with authority.*

Law students produce a lot of writing in law school. All law schools in the United States require first-year legal research and writing (LRW) courses that teach many professional legal genres: the client letter, the objective office memo, the persuasive appellate brief, and the oral argument, among others. Most law schools also require that students take at least one course in which they produce scholarly legal writing in the form of a seminar paper. The law school seminar paper is a work of legal scholarship on a timely legal topic that resembles the scholarly articles published in law journals. Sometimes, law students revise and publish these papers in law journals and reviews. This scholarly legal writing, conducted by law professors, judges, lawyers, and law students, has two primary functions: it *describes* how the law functions now and *prescribes* changes to the law (Volokh 9).

This book introduces nonlawyers to the basics of writing about law and of strong academic writing generally. You will learn to read and analyze primary legal documents such as cases, briefs, and statutes. You will learn how to use these documents in your academic writing and to cite them properly. You will also learn ways to share your research with others through presentations and publication in scholarly journals.

## Law Outside of Law Schools

A wide variety of disciplines—political science, history, sociology, criminal justice, to name a few—include courses in which you may be asked to explore U.S. law as part of a writing assignment. Why is law such an integral part of so many disciplines? There are three reasons:

- Law is a fascinating and wide-ranging field of research because it touches nearly all aspects of human relationships, public and private, business and personal.
- Law is ever changing and therefore ever in need of strong guidance from scholars who produce knowledgeable research. When you conduct your research and write a paper on a legal topic, your work might be of practical use to legal professionals.
- Study of law trains you to speak, read, write, and argue better than training in any other field or discipline. If you can read and write about law, you can read and write about anything.

## Citing Research

One major difference between writing about law in undergraduate courses—even pre-law courses—and writing for professional law journals is the style of legal citation. Legal writing, both professional and scholarly, uses a highly complex citation style called **Bluebook**, which is part of the core curriculum of law school LRW courses. Most university students who are not lawyers, however, should use the citation style recommended by their instructors. For convenience, this book uses Modern Language Association (MLA) and American Psychological Association (APA) styles, the styles most commonly used when nonlawyers write about law.

## THE U.S. LEGAL SYSTEM

An introduction to law requires an introduction to our legal system. The U.S. legal system is built on the early British legal system, which dates from the Middle Ages, and continues to share some commonalities with the contemporary British system (and systems used in other former British colonies like Canada and Australia). The most important similarity, the reliance on **common law**, means that previously decided cases, called **precedent**, are used to determine what the law is.

The common legal doctrine that says precedent should be followed is *stare decisis*, a Latin phrase meaning, "Let the decision stand." *Stare decisis* doctrine holds that courts should follow "the law as set forth in prior cases decided by the highest court of a given jurisdiction as long as the principle derived from those cases is logically essential to their decision, is reasonable, and is appropriate to contemporary circumstances" (Kempin 14). Because of *stare decisis*, lawyers use the prior decisions of our courts as support, or **authority**, for the legal arguments they make on behalf of their clients. In a common law legal system such as ours, then, the oldest type of authority is precedent, composed of prior court opinions, also called **case law**, because it is made through individual cases decided by judges.

U.S. law also derives from legal texts, materials, and procedures. The four primary **sources of law** are as follows:

- constitutions (both the federal Constitution and state constitutions);
- statutes, created by the legislative branches of state and federal governments and by city councils;
- administrative rules and executive orders, created by executive branches; and
- judge-made case law, created by the judicial branch (Dernbach 9).

Constitutions govern all other law, and the U.S. Constitution is the standard by which all legislation, both state and federal, is measured. Courts use the Constitution in order to determine whether a challenged statute or administrative rule is **unconstitutional**; the power held by the courts to say whether legislation violates the Constitution is called **judicial review**. When a court exercises judicial review, it compares a piece of legislation or an administrative rule with the Constitution (or a state constitution). If the court finds the law to be in conflict with the mandates of the Constitution, the court strikes down the law.

The cases mentioned in this book are, for the most part, U.S. Supreme Court cases that focus on constitutional law. In each of these cases, a person or group challenged the constitutionality of a particular law—school segregation on the basis of race, for example—and the Supreme Court determined whether the law violated the Constitution. This process of challenging laws in the courts is central to the function of our government. Table 1.1 offers an overview of the federal court system.

Table 1.1    The U.S. Federal Court System

| Type of Court | Function |
| --- | --- |
| U.S. district courts: the federal trial courts | District courts are the setting for two kinds of trials: (1) criminal trials, in which the government prosecutes an individual or group (the defendant) for violating a criminal law; and (2) civil trials, in which a private party (the plaintiff) sues another private party or the government (the defendant) for some violation of the plaintiff's interests. |
| U.S. courts of appeals: sometimes called **circuit courts**, includes twelve regional courts, plus the Federal Circuit Court, which has jurisdiction over special federal matters | A party dissatisfied with the result of a trial can **appeal**, or challenge, the district court's ruling in the circuit court. An appeal is not a new trial; rather, a panel of judges reviews the decision of the lower court to determine whether there were any legal problems with the procedures or outcome of the trial. The circuit court then issues a decision in the form of a written opinion. |
| U.S. Supreme Court | A party who disagrees with the circuit court's ruling may appeal to the U.S. Supreme Court, which hears only 1% of the cases people seek to bring before it. The justices choose to hear cases that, in their opinion, address the most pressing legal issues of the day. The Supreme Court's rulings are final—they can only be overturned by a future sitting of the Supreme Court. All lower courts, both state and federal, must abide by U.S. Supreme Court rulings. |

Most states have a similar structure for their court systems. Once a case reaches the highest court in an individual state, that court's decision can be appealed to the U.S. Supreme Court only if there is a federal issue in the case—in other words, if there is federal **jurisdiction** over the matter at hand. Some legal questions are solely the province of state courts. If a state court has sole jurisdiction over an issue, then the ruling of the state's highest court is the ultimate ruling on the issue, and all lower courts in that state must abide by the ruling.

The balance of power between the state and federal governments is tangled, delicate, and often fraught with controversy. Some jurisdiction is shared between the state and federal courts, and the parties can choose whether to bring suit in federal or state court. Sometimes the U.S. Supreme Court overrules a decision of a state supreme court or declares a state statute unconstitutional according to the federal Constitution, creating tension between federal and state governments. The case we examine later in this chapter, *Lawrence v. Texas* (2003), presents such a state–federal conflict. In *Lawrence*, the defendants asked the U.S. Supreme Court to declare certain state laws unconstitutional, and the Supreme Court agreed.

As you read this book and study cases, you may want to refer to the glossary of legal terms in the appendix. This section has looked at the structure and process of law; later, when you read cases, you will have examples of those processes at work. Studying law in action is the best way to learn about it, and the best way to study law in action is to read, study, and write about court opinions.

## RHETORIC AND LAW

The ability to identify and use the appropriate means of persuasion in any given situation—**rhetoric**—is an essential skill not only for lawyers, but also for academic writers in any discipline. Rhetoric governs every spoken, written, and new-media communication; it teaches that language is a public, political power. When lawyers argue before a judge, they exercise this power; when judges issue rulings, they too exercise this power. As a reader of and writer about law, you need to exercise this power, too. The remainder of this chapter will focus on helping you analyze legal arguments, frame scholarly legal arguments in your writing, and recognize when an argument is weak or strong—in other words, to apply rhetorical principles to law.

### Lawyers as Rhetoricians: The Sophists

The first rhetoricians and the first lawyers were one and the same. The **Sophists** of ancient Athens were rhetoric teachers; they trained citizens to argue their cases in court because laws forbade the use of hired advocates in courtrooms. Citizens hired these rhetoric teachers, who taught them how to assess a rhetorical situation, how to make strong arguments and identify weak ones, and how to convince audiences to decide in their favor.

The Sophists would teach rhetorical skills to anyone who could pay their fees and, as a result, were held in contempt by the Greek aristocracy. By teaching the lower classes how to argue, the Sophists gave them power—power the aristocracy did not want to share. Since the Sophists taught for money—sometimes a lot of money—the most successful of them grew very wealthy, earning a reputation for greed.

The bad reputation of the Athenian Sophists sounds a lot like the bad reputation of lawyers in the contemporary United States. Many Americans believe that lawyers are mercenaries—hired guns who will represent anyone able to pay their exorbitant fees. Sometimes we consider the work lawyers do to be unethical *manipulation*—using arguments to play on juries' emotions.

The important thing to learn from the Sophists, and from their bad reputation, is that *rhetoric is a tool*. It can be used for good or evil, just like any other tool. The mistrust of the Sophists, like the mistrust of lawyers, stems in part from a mistrust of the power of rhetoric. Let us learn more about that power.

## Genres of Oratory

Aristotle divided rhetorical speech into three types, or genres: forensic, political, and ceremonial. These genres offer a useful way to think about the purpose of a speech, legal argument, or other piece of communication.

- **Forensic oratory**, sometimes called *legal* or *judicial* oratory, seeks to discover what occurred in the past.
- **Political oratory**, often used by legislators when they debate law, seeks to discover the best way to resolve a current conflict.
- **Ceremonial oratory** is used mainly to praise or to cast blame on a person. A funeral eulogy is an example of ceremonial oratory, but it is also commonly used at political rallies by those who praise their candidates and cast aspersions on political opponents.

Lawyers (and most other speakers and writers) typically combine the three genres of oratory. For example, a defense lawyer might use forensic oratory to convince a jury that the defendant could not have been at the scene of a crime because he was visiting a family member in another city.

The lawyer will present evidence such as a train ticket that the defendant purchased and testimony of the defendant's family members claiming that he was staying in their home. The defense lawyer might use political oratory to appeal to the jury's sense of justice, arguing that they must acquit the defendant because to convict the defendant would violate his or her rights as a member of the community. Finally, a defense lawyer will use ceremonial oratory, often through the use of character witnesses, to persuade the jury that the defendant is a good and ethical person and therefore could not have committed a crime.

When writing about law, you need to be able to identify and assess the many arguments that lawyers, legislators, and judges make. You may use a variety of primary legal documents as sources for academic papers: court opinions, oral argument or trial transcripts, briefs written by the parties, statutes and other written rules, and the U.S. or state constitutions. These documents might appear complex and full of obscure language. If you examine these texts through the lens of rhetoric, however, you will find that they are not so difficult to understand. This examination is called **rhetorical analysis**.

## RHETORICAL ANALYSIS: THE RHETORICAL TRIANGLE

The first step in conducting a rhetorical analysis is to describe the rhetorical situation or context in which a text arose. In any rhetorical situation, there are three elements: a speaker, an audience, and a message—often referred to as the **rhetorical triangle**. In the triangle, all three points are equal, significant, and interdependent. In rhetorical terms, the *speaker* is trying to convince the *audience* to agree with the speaker's *message*.

In a criminal courtroom, the defense lawyer (speaker) tries to convince the jury (audience) to acquit the defendant. At the same time, the prosecutor (speaker) tries to convince the jury to convict the defendant. Both defense lawyer and prosecutor are offering messages, or arguments, designed to convince their audience.

In other legal settings, the rhetorical triangle may be less obvious, but it nevertheless exists: In a judicial opinion, the justice writing the opinion tries to convince an audience—the readers, who may be parties to a lawsuit, legal professionals, and even the general citizenry—that the court's opinion is correct. A legal scholar tries to convince readers that a particular scholarly argument about law is correct. The rhetorical triangle is central to much of the work that lawyers, judges, and legal scholars do.

Table 1.2    The Rhetorical Triangle

| | |
|---|---|
| **Speaker** | Who is the speaker? How does she present herself? Is she reliable? Does she have authority? How does she establish that authority—in other words, what reasons does she give (either directly or indirectly) to convince you to listen to her and believe what she says? |
| **Audience** | Who is the intended audience of the communication? Does the speaker name the audience in some way? Might there be unintended audiences? Can you list all of the possible audiences of this communication? What might each audience, in particular, find persuasive in the speaker's arguments? |
| **Message** | What is the message of the communication? What is the purpose? What is the speaker trying to convince the audience of? Is there an action that the speaker hopes the audience will take after listening to the communication? |

Basing your analysis of legal documents on the rhetorical triangle can help you understand the arguments being used. Table 1.2 provides a useful set of questions to help you apply the rhetorical triangle to a legal document.

What follows is an excerpt from a U.S. Supreme Court opinion from 2003, *Lawrence v. Texas.* (Since we will return to this case throughout this book, you may want to read it carefully.) In *Lawrence*, the court voted 6-to-3 to strike down a Texas crime-against-nature law. *Crime-against-nature laws*, sometimes called *sodomy laws*, were common in U.S. state statutes until the mid-twentieth century. These statutes defined some sexual acts as crimes, punishable with fines, prison sentences, or both. The laws were often used to target homosexual persons. By 2003, all but fifteen states had repealed their crime-against-nature laws. The *Lawrence* decision declared any remaining laws unconstitutional, thereby invalidating the statutes of the fifteen states.

The Supreme Court produced three opinions in this case:

- Justice Anthony Kennedy wrote the opinion for the majority, which held that crime-against-nature laws violate the Due Process Clause of the Fourteenth Amendment of the U.S. Constitution.
- Justice Sandra Day O'Connor wrote a concurring opinion in which she reached the same conclusion as the majority—that crime-against-nature laws violate the Constitution—but she based

her decision on the equal protection clause rather than the due process clause.

- Justice Antonin Scalia wrote a dissenting opinion on behalf of himself and the two other dissenting justices. He argued that the laws should not have struck down the state laws. (Justice Clarence Thomas also wrote a dissenting opinion, but his opinion has not been included in this book.)

As you read excerpts from these three opinions, keep in mind the rhetorical triangle questions from Table 1.2.

One last note: Judicial opinions are published in books called **law reports**, or **reporters**. Publishers of judicial opinions typically refer to these volumes when reprinting or excerpting opinions, and those references are included in brackets in the text. The *Lawrence* opinion appears in volume 539 of the *U.S. Reporter*, beginning on page 558. The brackets in the following case indicate where the pages begin and end in the *U.S. Reporter*.

---

### *Lawrence v. Texas*, 539 U.S. 558 (2003)

[539 U.S. 562]

#### Justice Kennedy Delivered the Opinion of the Court.

Liberty protects the person from unwarranted government intrusions into a dwelling or other private places. In our tradition the State is not omnipresent in the home. And there are other spheres of our lives and existence, outside the home, where the State should not be a dominant presence. Freedom extends beyond spatial bounds. Liberty presumes an autonomy of self that includes freedom of thought, belief, expression, and certain intimate conduct. The instant case involves liberty of the person both in its spatial and in its more transcendent dimensions.

The question before the Court is the validity of a Texas statute making it a crime for two persons of the same sex to engage in certain intimate sexual conduct.

In Houston, Texas, officers of the Harris County Police Department were dispatched to a private residence in response to a reported weapons disturbance. They entered an apartment where one of the petitioners, John Geddes Lawrence, [539 U.S. 563] resided. The right of the police to enter does not seem to have been questioned. The officers observed Lawrence and another

*(Continued)*

man, Tyron Garner, engaging in a sexual act. The two petitioners were arrested, held in custody overnight, and charged and convicted before a Justice of the Peace.

The complaints described their crime as "deviate sexual intercourse, namely anal sex, with a member of the same sex (man).". . . The applicable state law . . . provides: "A person commits an offense if he engages in deviate sexual intercourse with another individual of the same sex.". . .

[539 U.S. 564] We conclude the case should be resolved by determining whether the petitioners were free as adults to engage in the private conduct in the exercise of their liberty under the Due Process Clause of the Fourteenth Amendment to the Constitution. For this inquiry we deem it necessary to reconsider the Court's holding in *Bowers*.

There are broad statements of the substantive reach of liberty under the Due Process Clause in earlier cases . . . but the most pertinent beginning point is our decision in *Griswold v. Connecticut*, 381 U. S. 479 (1965).

In *Griswold* the Court invalidated a state law prohibiting the use of drugs or devices of contraception and counseling or aiding and abetting the use of contraceptives. The Court described the protected interest as a right to privacy and [539 U.S. 565] placed emphasis on the marriage relation and the protected space of the marital bedroom.

After *Griswold* it was established that the right to make certain decisions regarding sexual conduct extends beyond the marital relationship. In *Eisenstadt v. Baird*, 405 U. S. 438 (1972), the Court invalidated a law prohibiting the distribution of contraceptives to unmarried persons. . . .

The opinions in *Griswold* and *Eisenstadt* were part of the background for the decision in *Roe v. Wade*, 410 U. S. 113 (1973). As is well known, the case involved a challenge to the Texas law prohibiting abortions, but the laws of other States were affected as well. Although the Court held the woman's rights were not absolute, her right to elect an abortion did have real and substantial protection as an exercise of her liberty under the Due Process Clause. . . .

[539 U.S. 566] This was the state of the law with respect to some of the most relevant cases when the Court considered *Bowers v. Hardwick*.

The facts in *Bowers* had some similarities to the instant case. A police officer, whose right to enter seems not to have been in question, observed Hardwick, in his own bedroom, engaging in intimate sexual conduct with another adult male. The conduct was in violation of a Georgia statute making it a criminal offense to engage in sodomy. One difference between the two cases is that the Georgia statute prohibited the conduct whether or not the participants were of the same sex, while the Texas statute, as we have seen, applies only to participants of the same sex. Hardwick was not prosecuted, but he brought an action in federal court to declare the state statute invalid. He alleged he was a practicing homosexual and that the criminal prohibition violated rights guaranteed to him by the Constitution. The Court, in an opinion by Justice White, sustained the Georgia law. . . .

The Court began its substantive discussion in *Bowers* as follows: "The issue presented is whether the Federal Constitution confers a fundamental right upon homosexuals to engage in sodomy and hence invalidates the laws of the many States that still make such conduct illegal and have done so [539 U.S. 567] for a very long time." That statement, we now conclude, discloses the Court's own failure to appreciate the extent of the liberty at stake. To say that the issue in *Bowers* was simply the right to engage in certain sexual conduct demeans the claim the individual put forward, just as it would demean a married couple were it to be said marriage is simply about the right to have sexual intercourse. The laws involved in *Bowers* and here are, to be sure, statutes that purport to do no more than prohibit a particular sexual act. Their penalties and purposes, though, have more far-reaching consequences, touching upon the most private human conduct, sexual behavior, and in the most private of places, the home. The statutes do seek to control a personal relationship that, whether or not entitled to formal recognition in the law, is within the liberty of persons to choose without being punished as criminals . . .

It suffices for us to acknowledge that adults may choose to enter upon this relationship in the confines of their homes and their own private lives and still retain their dignity as free persons. When sexuality finds overt expression in intimate conduct with another person, the conduct can be but one element in a personal bond that

*(Continued)*

is more enduring. The liberty protected by the Constitution allows homosexual persons the right to make this choice. . . .

[539 U.S. 568] At the outset it should be noted that there is no longstanding history in this country of laws directed at homosexual conduct as a distinct matter. Beginning in colonial times there were prohibitions of sodomy derived from the English criminal laws passed in the first instance by the Reformation Parliament in 1533. The English prohibition was understood to include relationship between men and women as well as relations between men and men. . . .

[539 U.S. 570] It was not until the 1970's that any State singled out same-sex relations for criminal prosecution, and only nine States have done so. . . .

[539 U.S. 576] To the extent *Bowers* relied on values we share with a wider civilization, it should be noted that the reasoning and holding in *Bowers* have been rejected elsewhere. The European Court of Human Rights has followed not *Bowers* but its own decision in *Dudgeon v. United Kingdom* [in which the ECHR held that laws forbidding consensual homosexual conduct were invalid]. Other nations, too, have taken action consistent with an affirmation of the protected right of homosexual adults to engage in intimate, consensual conduct. [539 U.S. 577] The right the petitioners seek in this case has been accepted as an integral part of human freedom in many other countries. . . .

[539 U.S. 578] *Bowers* was not correct when it was decided, and it is not correct today. It ought not to remain binding precedent. *Bowers v. Hardwick* should be and now is overruled.

[The Lawrence case] does involve two adults who, with full and mutual consent from each other, engaged in sexual practices common to a homosexual lifestyle. The petitioners are entitled to respect for their private lives. The State cannot demean their existence or control their destiny by making their private sexual conduct a crime. Their right to liberty under the Due Process Clause gives them the full right to engage in their conduct without intervention of the government. . . .

[539 U.S. 579] The judgment of the Court of Appeals for the Texas Fourteenth District is reversed, and the case is remanded for further proceedings not inconsistent with this opinion. It is so ordered.

## Justice O'Connor, Concurring in the Judgment.

The Court today overrules *Bowers v. Hardwick*, 478 U.S. 186 (1986). I joined *Bowers*, and do not join the Court in overruling it. Nevertheless, I agree with the Court that Texas' statute banning same-sex sodomy is unconstitutional. Rather than relying on the substantive component of the Fourteenth Amendment's Due Process Clause, as the Court does, I base my conclusion on the Fourteenth Amendment's Equal Protection Clause. . . .

[539 U.S. 581] The statute at issue here makes sodomy a crime only if a person "engages in deviate sexual intercourse with another individual of the same sex." Sodomy between opposite-sex partners, however, is not a crime in Texas. That is, Texas treats the same conduct differently based solely on the participants. Those harmed by this law are people who have a same-sex sexual orientation and thus are more likely to engage in behavior prohibited by [the Texas statute].

The Texas statute makes homosexuals unequal in the eyes of the law by making particular conduct—and only that conduct— subject to criminal sanction. . . .

[539 U.S. 586]

## Justice Scalia, with whom the Chief Justice [Rehnquist] and Justice Thomas Join, Dissenting.

. . . I begin with the Court's surprising readiness to reconsider a decision rendered a mere 17 years ago in *Bowers v. Hardwick* [539 U.S. 587]. I do not myself believe in rigid adherence to *stare decisis* in constitutional cases; but I do believe that we should be consistent rather than manipulative in invoking the doctrine. Today's opinions in support of reversal do not bother to distinguish—or indeed, even bother to mention—the paean to stare decisis coauthored by three Members of today's majority in *Planned Parenthood v. Casey*. There, when *stare decisis* meant preservation of judicially invented abortion rights, the widespread criticism of *Roe* was a strong reason to reaffirm it. . . .

[539 U.S. 590] State laws against bigamy, same-sex marriage, adult incest, prostitution, masturbation, adultery, fornication, bestiality, and obscenity are likewise sustainable only in light of *Bowers'* validation of laws based on moral choices. Every

*(Continued)*

single one of these laws is called into question by today's decisions; the Court makes no effort to cabin the scope of its decisions to exclude them from its holding. . . .

[539 U.S. 605] The matters appropriate for this Court's resolution are only three: Texas's prohibition of sodomy neither infringes a "fundamental right" (which the Court does not dispute), nor is unsupported by a rational relation to what the Constitution considers a legitimate state interest, nor denies equal protection of the laws. I dissent.

## *Lawrence v. Texas* and the Rhetorical Triangle

Let us examine the *Lawrence* opinion using the analytical tools provided by the rhetorical triangle.

**Speaker(s)**   The speakers in this excerpt are Justices Kennedy, O'Connor, and Scalia, but Kennedy and Scalia also wrote on behalf of other justices (Kennedy for the majority, including four other justices, and Scalia for two other dissenting justices). In this case, there is another implied speaker as well: the U.S. Supreme Court, and, in turn, the U.S. government, of which the Supreme Court is an arm. We might even argue that the speaker is the people of the United States, for whom their government speaks.

**Audience(s)**   The audiences for a Supreme Court opinion are also many and include the following:

- the parties to the case, Lawrence and Garner, who challenged their convictions under the Texas statute;
- the government of the state of Texas, which defended its statute;
- the people of the state of Texas, whose law is being overturned;
- the people of the fifteen other states whose "crime-against-nature" statutes will be invalidated as well;
- all homosexual persons living in the United States, whose lives may be directly affected;
- all U.S. citizens who are interested in the governance of this country.

**Message(s)**   The primary message of a case is called the **holding**, also known as the **ruling**, which is a clear statement of the case's legal effect. The holding is the *actual legal decision* made by the court; here, the holding is that crime-against-nature laws violate the due process clause of the U.S. Constitution and are therefore invalid. However, the case had many other messages:

- The majority ruled that certain sexual conduct should be free from governmental intrusion—in other words, that sexual freedom is an important right. "Liberty presumes an autonomy of self that includes freedom of thought, belief, expression, and certain intimate conduct" (562).
- The majority also overruled *Bowers v. Hardwick* (1986), an earlier Supreme Court challenge to crime-against-nature laws, declaring, "*Bowers* was not correct when it was decided, and it is not correct today" (578).
- A final point with regard to the majority opinion is that it also carried a message that homosexual persons should not be punished as criminals and the implication that homosexuality is not a crime.
- Justice Scalia, on the other hand, attacked the majority's legal reasoning in overturning *Bowers*, suggesting that the court is applying the doctrine of *stare decisis* inconsistently (587). He also argued that *Lawrence* will have far-reaching consequences because states will no longer be able to make laws "based on moral choices" (590).

## RHETORICAL APPEALS

Once you have identified the rhetorical context—that is, the three corners of the rhetorical triangle—in a given situation, you will want to evaluate whether the speaker's arguments are valid. A speaker persuades his audience using three **rhetorical appeals**, categorized by Aristotle. Table 1.3 describes each appeal.

Now, let us examine the *Lawrence* opinions through the lens of rhetorical appeals, looking at each appeal in turn.

First, Justice Kennedy, the author of the opinion, has great authority (*ethos*) because he is a Supreme Court justice. Whether or not we agree with the perspectives of the justices, most Americans agree that all nine justices are very intelligent and knowledgeable in law.

Kennedy also derives authority in this particular case because his is considered by many to be a politically conservative justice. He was appointed to the court by Republican president Ronald Reagan in 1988, and in other cases before the court, he has often voted in agreement with other politically conservative justices, such as former Chief Justice Rehnquist

Table 1.3   The Rhetorical Appeals

| | |
|---|---|
| *Ethos* | An appeal based on the personal character of the speaker. A reliable, authoritative *ethos* suggests that the audience should believe that the speaker is an ethical, trustworthy, and credible authority on the subject at hand. For example, lawyers use *ethos* when they speak confidently and authoritatively to a jury in a manner designed to gain the jurors' trust. A judge writing an opinion creates an authoritative *ethos* by illustrating strong legal expertise, which supports the ruling. English words derived from *ethos* are *ethical* and *ethics*. |
| *Pathos* | An appeal based on putting the audience into a certain frame of mind. A speaker employs *pathos* by appealing to the audience's emotions in order to change their view of a case. Use of *pathos* requires that the speaker understand human emotions in order to evoke them in the audience. For example, prosecutors use *pathos* when they try to evoke the jury's anger toward criminal defendants in order to get harsher sentences. Defense lawyers use it by putting positive character witnesses on the stand. English words derived from *pathos* are *sympathetic*, *empathetic*, and *pathetic*. |
| *Logos* | An appeal based on proofs. A speaker employs *logos* using logical reasoning, factual evidence, and reliable sources. When lawyers or judges make an arguments based on strong research, using excellent legal authority cited correctly, they rely on *logos*. When defense attorneys present physical evidence at trial to acquit clients, they are using *logos*. English words derived from *logos* are *logical* and *logistics*. |

and Justices Scalia and Thomas—all three of whom dissented in *Lawrence*. Of the five justices who composed the majority in *Lawrence*, then, Kennedy was the most politically conservative. This makes him an excellent candidate to author the opinion because his vote for homosexual rights does not appear to be politically motivated. Instead, he appears driven by what we might call *justice*. Kennedy establishes this politically neutral *ethos* when he writes, "The instant case involves liberty of the person both in its spatial and in its more transcendent dimensions" (562). Kennedy insists that "liberty," not partisan politics, drives his opinion.

In the first paragraph of the opinion, Kennedy makes an appeal to *pathos*: "Liberty protects the person from unwarranted government intrusions into a dwelling or other private places. In our tradition the State is not omnipresent in the home" (562). In this paragraph, by implying that the law at issue in the case violates "liberty"—a concept that Americans hold dear, one we often call *freedom*—Kennedy earns readers' emotional support.

Kennedy also appeals to *pathos* when he mentions the "home," invoking the protective feelings most of us have toward our living places. He appeals once more to *pathos* when he writes, "When sexuality finds overt expression in intimate conduct with another person, the conduct can be but one element in a personal bond that is more enduring. The liberty protected by the Constitution allows homosexual persons the right to make this choice" (567). Here, he appeals to our common experiences of human emotional and physical bonding, arguing that homosexuals should have the freedom to love and touch one another just as heterosexuals do.

Kennedy also makes appeals to *logos*. When he points to earlier cases such as *Griswold v. Connecticut, Eisenstadt v. Baird*, and *Roe v. Wade*, he is claiming that these powerful Supreme Court opinions support the majority holding in *Lawrence*. Few would argue that adults do not have the freedom to use birth control, as established by *Griswold* and *Eisenstadt*. By claiming that the right at stake in *Lawrence* is the same as that of these earlier cases, Kennedy uses case law to build a logical foundation for the majority opinion.

What we have done in the foregoing paragraphs—using the lenses of rhetorical context and appeals to analyze a court opinion—is an example of rhetorical analysis. Writing a rhetorical analysis is an effective way to examine a court opinion because it encourages you to look at each argument in detail and to study the language closely. Such close analysis will allow you to identify weak arguments, such as ones that do not appropriately address their audience or that are not supported by valid proofs.

## MAKING VALID ARGUMENTS: SYLLOGISMS AND FALLACIES

A **syllogism** is the basic structure of a formal, logical argument. It has three parts:

1. a major premise, which is usually a generally agreed-upon claim;
2. a minor premise, which is an argument that pertains to the speaker's particular context; and
3. a conclusion, which brings together the major and minor premises into the speaker's new argument.

A **fallacy** is an argument whose *logic fails*, or whose *premises are weak or untrue*. Consider, for example, this argument:

**Major Premise:** Dogs make good pets.
**Minor Premise:** Poodles are dogs.
**Conclusion:** Poodles make good pets.

In this instance, the first statement—the major premise—is simply not true: *All* dogs do *not* make good pets. It may be true that *some* dogs make good pets, and the minor premise, that poodles are dogs, is certainly true. However, because the major premise is flawed, the conclusion is too. To be more accurate, the major premise should read "Some dogs make good pets." We have solved the problem of a weak premise.

If this is our new major premise, can we rephrase the conclusion so that it follows logically from the premises? What if we say that some poodles do indeed make good pets, but others may not? Can the premises sustain the conclusion, "Some poodles make good pets?" The answer is *no*. We have no way of knowing whether any poodles at all fall into the group of dogs that make good pets. They might *all* fall into the "not-good-pets" category. We now have a failure of logic.

Legal arguments are replete with syllogisms and fallacies. Legal writing professor Ruth McKinney writes that syllogistic reasoning "is the heart and soul of clear legal thinking." She suggests that we think of the parts of a syllogism used in legal reasoning in this way: The major premise is the "rule" of a legal situation; the minor premise is the "facts"; the conclusion follows when the rule is applied to facts (McKinney 35).

Let us look at an example of this type of reasoning. Like most Supreme Court opinions, *Lawrence* contains some strong arguments and some weak arguments. For example, when Kennedy lists earlier Supreme Court cases that he claims support the holding in *Lawrence*, he includes *Roe v. Wade* (1973). *Roe* held that state laws banning abortion are unconstitutional. Kennedy relies on *Roe* because it is an important precedent in establishing privacy rights under the Constitution, and this "right to privacy" is the law Kennedy relies on in *Lawrence*. The syllogism can be drawn like this:

**Major Premise:** *Roe v. Wade* is good law.
**Minor Premise:** *Lawrence v. Texas* is similar to *Roe v. Wade*.
**Conclusion:** *Lawrence v. Texas* is good law.

The major premise, that *Roe* is good law, is the "rule" that Kennedy applies. The similarity between *Lawrence* and *Roe* is the fact specific to this particular case. The conclusion, that *Lawrence* is also good law, is the conclusion that results from applying the major premise to the minor premise.

Here is one problem with this syllogism: Many lawyers, judges, and legal scholars—even those that support abortion rights—believe that *Roe* is not good law at all. Some suggest that *Roe* lacks strong constitutional support. Others argue that it depends on the reproductive science of the 1970s, science that is now outdated. Thus, some might consider the major premise weak and thereby the conclusion weak as well.

The minor premise might also have its detractors. One might suggest that *Lawrence* and *Roe* are not similar at all—or at least, not similar in any relevant respect. This would make our minor premise a *weak analogy*, which also makes our conclusion weak.

Since Kennedy also lists other cases that *are* considered good law by a vast majority of legal professionals—*Griswold v. Connecticut*, for example—many agree that Kennedy's upholding of *Lawrence* based on the due process clause is appropriately supported.

## Hidden Premises: Enthymemes

Kennedy never explicitly states that *Roe* is good law. Instead, he leaves the major premise out of his syllogism, pointing instead to the general soundness of the many cases he lists. Kennedy uses an **enthymeme**, a type of syllogism common to persuasive public speaking and writing. An enthymeme is simply a syllogism in which a premise is left unspoken or unwritten—a syllogism with a missing premise, usually a missing major premise, one that the audience can fill in using shared knowledge.

Why should a speaker use an enthymeme instead of a complete syllogism? Sometimes, the major premise is so obvious that it does not need to be stated. In this type of situation, a speaker may leave out the major premise simply to keep the audience engaged by letting them fill in the blanks. This can be particularly effective if there are several obvious potential major premises; leaving them out allows each member of the audience to settle on the one that each finds most compelling.

Other times, however, the speaker knowingly relies on a major premise that is untrue, unpersuasive, or unpleasant, and the speaker leaves it out in order to hide a rhetorical fallacy.

## Enthymemes in Action

The author of the following news article, political insider Richard A. Davis, directed John McCain's 2000 campaign for the Republican presidential nomination—a campaign that ended with the nomination of George W. Bush. The article describes a common campaign tactic called a "push poll." Read Davis's description of a push poll run by the Bush campaign against McCain.

- What is the major premise hidden in the arguments of the push-pollsters?
- Can you think of more than one premise?
- Do you agree with their arguments? Why or why not?

### "The Anatomy of a Smear Campaign"

*by Richard A. Davis*
*The Boston Globe, March 21, 2004*

Having run Senator John McCain's campaign for president, I can recount a textbook example of a smear made against McCain in South Carolina during the 2000 presidential primary. We had just swept into the state from New Hampshire, where we had racked up a shocking, 19-point win over the heavily favored George W. Bush. What followed was a primary campaign that would make history for its negativity. . . .

It didn't take much research to turn up a seemingly innocuous fact about the McCains: [they have an adopted Bangladeshi daughter named Bridget].

Anonymous opponents used "push polling" to suggest that McCain's Bangladeshi born daughter was his own, illegitimate black child. In push polling, a voter gets a call, ostensibly from a polling company, asking which candidate the voter supports. In this case, if the "pollster" determined that the person was a McCain supporter, he made statements designed to create doubt about the senator.

Thus, the "pollsters" asked McCain supporters if they would be more or less likely to vote for McCain if they knew he had fathered an illegitimate child who was black. In the conservative, race-conscious South, that's not a minor charge. We had no idea who made the phone calls, who paid for them, or how many calls were made. Effective and anonymous: the perfect smear campaign. . . .

"The Anatomy of a Smear Campaign" by Richard Davis, *The Boston Globe*, March 24, 2004. Reprinted with kind permission of Richard Davis.

Let us try to map out the syllogism of the push-pollsters, working backward from the conclusion.

**Conclusion:** South Carolinians should not vote for McCain.

**Minor Premise:** John McCain might have fathered an interracial child.

**Major Premise:** ?

The major premise, it appears, could be either "Fathering an interracial child makes a man unfit to be president," or more simply, "Fathering an interracial child is bad." The push-pollsters hid this racist major premise in an enthymeme.

Here is another example of a hidden weak major premise, this time from the courtroom. Johnnie Cochran, a famous defense attorney, represented O. J. Simpson in his murder trial in the mid-1990s. Early in the trial, the prosecution argued that a bloody leather glove found at the scene belonged to the murderer of Nicole Brown Simpson and Ron Goldman. At Cochran's urging, Simpson tried on the glove, and it was noticeably tight on his hand. In his closing arguments to the jury, Cochran uttered the most famous phrase of the trial: "If [the glove] doesn't fit, you must acquit." Mapped as an enthymeme, conclusion first, here is Cochran's argument:

**Conclusion:** Simpson is not guilty of the murders.

**Minor Premise:** The glove does not fit Simpson.

**Major Premise:** ?

The missing major premise appears to be, "The murderer wore this glove during the murders." The elegance of Cochran's courtroom argument is that Cochran did not frame the flawed major premise himself; the prosecutors did it for him when they presented the glove as evidence. Because Cochran never presented the major premise, he employed an enthymeme.

How is Cochran's major premise flawed? There are a number of ways. Perhaps the murderer was rushed and agitated when purchasing the gloves and ended up with a pair that was too small for him. Perhaps the murderer borrowed the glove from a friend with smaller hands. Perhaps the glove had shrunk after being saturated with the blood of the victims.

However, Cochran's argument was powerful—and Simpson was acquitted.

## WRITING A FORMAL RHETORICAL ANALYSIS

Rhetorical analysis is the most effective way for nonlawyers to understand and assess legal arguments. In fact, analysis of arguments using rhetorical tools is one of the functions of legal scholarship—even if legal scholars rarely use the term "rhetoric." When scholars read court opinions closely and critically and measure the strengths of the arguments, they are analyzing that opinion rhetorically.

Many fields use rhetorical analysis: Marketing and advertising professionals come quickly to mind, as do lawyers. Although these professionals may not produce written rhetorical analyses, their examination of audience, speaker, and message—and of *ethos*, *pathos*, and *logos*—is similar. As you study court opinions, you may find it useful to write rhetorical analyses. These analyses will help you learn to read court opinions and assess the arguments that judges use to support rulings. Remember, in a rhetorical analysis, it is your job not only to outline the persuasive elements of the opinion, but also to *assess* the strengths and weaknesses of these elements.

You might find it useful to remind yourself of rhetorical structure by using three headings in your text—Speaker/*Ethos*, Audience/*Pathos*, and Message/*Logos*. Under each heading, you should identify the rhetorical situation and then discuss the persuasive value of each appeal. Before the first heading, you should write a short introductory paragraph outlining the main arguments of your analysis.

Here are some suggestions for writing a strong rhetorical analysis of a judicial opinion.

## What Is the Context?

After reading the court opinion you are to analyze, you need to identify the parties and the historical context in which the legal conflict arose. You should also try to discover more about the judge or judges who authored the opinion. Be sure you understand all of the legal terms and concepts mentioned in the opinion.

## Who Is Talking?

Write a paragraph or two about the speaker and whether the speaker has adopted an effective *ethos*. (Remember, sometimes there is more than one speaker.) It is not enough simply to provide a biography; you must draw connections between the speaker's biography and the success or failure of the piece of rhetoric. You should also evaluate the rhetorical techniques the speaker uses to cultivate a reliable *ethos*—to establish expertise, authority, and credibility.

## Are You Moved?

When writing about audience, list all of the possible audiences to whom this message is addressed, as well as those that might have encountered this message beyond the intent of the speaker.

Rhetoricians sometimes call these different audiences the "named audience," the "implied audience," the "intended audience," and the "unintended audience."

Recall that in our analysis of *Lawrence v. Texas*, there were many audiences—the parties to the case, the state of Texas, homosexual persons, and the entire population of the United States.

You should also consider whether the speaker appeals to the audience's emotions or feelings and how a particular audience might react to such appeals. Are there any arguments that you find particularly moving? Why? Are there other audiences that might be moved by these arguments?

## Are the Arguments Valid?

Ask yourself: Which arguments in this opinion are strong? Which ones are weak? Why? *Give reasons* for your assessments and *quote the text* of the opinion to prove your point.

Are there any fallacious arguments? Is the major premise of each argument always stated or obvious? Try writing out some arguments in the form of syllogisms and examine the strength of the premises relied on by the conclusions.

It is your job, as the writer of a rhetorical analysis, to provide more than just a summary of the communication. You must also provide critical assessment, examining the effectiveness of the communication. This critical analysis will be very important as you start writing scholarly legal research.

### Rhetorical Analysis Checklist

- Did you present a summary of your analysis at the beginning, including a thesis statement?
- Did you name all of the speakers of the opinion?
- Did you assess the credibility and authority (*ethos*) of the speaker(s)?
- Did you name all of the possible audiences (intended, unintended, named, etc.)?
- Did you identify all of the ways in which the speaker(s) tries to persuade each audience?
- Did you identify the ways in which the speaker(s) attempts to use emotional persuasion?
- Did you list all of the arguments made by the speaker(s)?
- Did you assess whether these arguments are strong or weak?
- Are there any rhetorical fallacies in the speaker's arguments? Are they formal or informal?

# 2

# READING CASES

## WHAT ARE CASES AND OPINIONS?

In order to read a case or an opinion, we need to understand what these things actually are. Confusion arises because these words can refer to a variety of legal documents and events.

In general, the term **case** refers to any conflict between two or more parties that has entered the legal system. A case may enter the legal system when one party sues another party or when the police arrest a person for committing a crime. Sometimes a case ends very quickly: The lawsuit settles out of court or the defendant makes a plea bargain. Sometimes, though, the resolution of a case takes years.

First, there may be a trial in front of a judge and/or a jury. If a party is unhappy with the process or outcome of the trial, then the party can appeal the verdict to a **court of appeals**, a higher court composed of judges who review what happened during trial. Thus, an appeal occurs when a party challenges the decision of a court by asking a higher court to review the decision. Sometimes a party can appeal the ruling by the court of appeals to an even higher court of appeals. The highest court in the United States is the U.S. Supreme Court. (See Chapter 1 for more on the state and federal court systems.)

Let us return to *Lawrence v. Texas* (2003) and study how this case progressed through the courts. (The text of the opinion appears in Chapter 1.)

- The case first arose in 1998, when John Lawrence and his co-defendant Tyron Garner were arrested near Houston, Texas, for violating the Texas crime-against-nature statute. At an informal criminal hearing they were convicted by a justice of the peace. Their punishment was a fine of $200 plus court costs.

- Under Texas law, defendants have a right to request a full trial in the criminal court, a right Lawrence and Garner exercised after their first guilty verdict. At their full criminal trial, they challenged the validity of the charges against them, claiming that the statute violated the Fourteenth Amendment of the U.S. Constitution. The criminal court judge denied their motion to dismiss the charges and convicted them again.

- They appealed the decision to a Texas court of appeals, again arguing that the statute violated the Constitution. This Texas court of appeals voted 7–2 to uphold the conviction. The highest appeals court in Texas refused to hear the case.

- Lawrence and Garner—who we should now call the **appellants** because they are the appealing party—then filed an appeal with the U.S. Supreme Court, which agreed to hear the case in 2002. The Supreme Court issued its opinion in *Lawrence* in 2003, declaring the Texas statute, and all other states' crime-against-nature statutes, unconstitutional.

This story of how *Lawrence v. Texas* progressed through the courts is called the **procedural history** of the case. When you study a case, you should study the procedural history as well, in order to understand how a case originated.

Let us review. Cases begin in one of two ways. A person is arrested, or a person files a lawsuit. If a person is arrested, the case goes to criminal court. If a person files a lawsuit against another person or entity, the case goes to civil court. Sometimes the case ends before or at trial. Sometimes the case is appealed to a higher court. All of the different hearings and trials that are described in the procedural history of *Lawrence* are part of the *Lawrence* case. The *Lawrence* case thus includes two criminal trials, a Texas appeals court hearing, a denial of hearing by a higher Texas appeals court, and then a hearing by the U.S. Supreme Court.

After an appeals court hears a case, the judges or justices issue a written **opinion** in which they provide a holding on the matter before the court. The opinion is a document written by one or more judges of the court, analyzing the issues of the case and explaining why the court held the way it did. The holding is the actual legal decision the court makes and can usually be summarized in a single sentence. Opinions, on the other hand, can be hundreds of pages long.

# ELEMENTS OF A CASE BRIEF

For every case you study, you should write a case brief. A **case brief** is an outline of the important parts of an appellate court opinion. You break the opinion into its primary components and analyze them separately. Law students use case briefs to prepare for exams. Lawyers use case briefs to prepare legal arguments for court. Legal scholars use case briefs to study the effectiveness of the arguments of a case and to prepare to write about these arguments.

According to legal writing expert Ruth McKinney, a case brief is "a tool that law students, law professors, and lawyers can use to help organize the information presented in legal opinions in a way that makes that information manageable and easy to retrieve" (19). Essentially, a case brief creates a framework for understanding an opinion's complex parts.

Case briefs, like judicial opinions, follow a specific format. There are six main parts of a brief. When you brief cases in preparation for your research, try to write them in the format to be provided below. Later in life, if you go to law school or practice law, you can adjust the format to best fit your needs. A case brief should have subheadings in bold or capital letters that correspond to the sections listed below. Complete sentences are not necessary and can be unhelpful; you need to be able to find the pertinent information quickly.

You should strive to write the brief in your words rather than quote the opinion. Translating the court opinion into your words is essential to learning law. As Ruth McKinney suggests, writing a case brief in your words is "the best way to use a case brief to forward your understanding of the law" (177). This is because "[w]riting out your thoughts forces you to bring them to a conscious level and identify what you don't yet understand." There is an exception to this rule, however. If the court uses a special word or legal phrase that you really want to remember, you should quote it in your brief. An example of this type of special phrase is "separate, but equal" from the race segregation case *Plessy v. Ferguson* (1896).

Let us now examine the components of a case brief.

## Case Name and Citation

**Case names** are the titles of legal cases, composed of the names of the parties separated by a "v." Case names are also complicated. In general, a case has three different names: the full name, the abbreviated full name, and the short name. The full name is the complete listing of all of the parties to a case, exactly how they appear on the text of the court filings. For example, the *Lawrence* case's full title looks like this: *John Geddes Lawrence and Tyron Garner, Petitioners v. Texas*. Lawrence and Garner are called **petitioners** because they petitioned the Supreme Court to hear their case. The state of Texas, in *Lawrence*, is the **respondent** because it is responding to the petition.

Legal writers rarely use the full name of a case. The full name is important for official record keeping. Most of the time, however, legal writers use the abbreviated full name. This is the name that most people are familiar with: *Lawrence v. Texas*. Do not just make up an abbreviated full name for a case. Instead, use the one that lawyers, scholars, and courts use. Whenever you refer to a case in your writing for the first time, you should use the abbreviated full name and give the date of the opinion in parentheses. After you have established the abbreviated full name of the case in your text, you can start using the short name if you wish.

The short name is a one-word abbreviation of the case name, for example, when we refer to *Lawrence v. Texas* as "*Lawrence*." Short names are created by common use. Sometimes the first party's name becomes the short name. We use "*Lawrence*" because it would be silly to call the case "*Texas*," which could refer to hundreds, even thousands, of cases in which the state of Texas is a party. Remember to only use the short name in your writing *after* you have established the abbreviated full title of the case. If the short name might cause confusion in your writing, you should stick to the abbreviated full name. (For more on using case names in your writing, see Chapter 6.)

There are two formatting notes to remember when writing case names. First, always italicize the name, no matter which form of the name you use. Case names should be treated like the titles of books for the purposes of formatting. In most formatting styles, book titles are either italicized or underlined in written text. Always refer to the formatting rule of the style you are using (e.g., MLA, *Chicago Manual of Style*, APA).

Second, avoid "vs." when referring to legal cases. Case names always use "v." Although both "v." and "vs." are abbreviations for "versus," only boxing matches use "vs." So, *Tyson vs. Holyfield* is a boxing match; *Holyfield v. Tyson* is a fictional lawsuit in which Evander Holyfield sues Mike Tyson for personal injuries sustained when Tyson bit off a part of his ear in their 1997 rematch.

After you have written the title correctly in your case brief, you must next write the **case citation**. The citation is a series of letters and numbers that tell lawyers and scholars where the opinion is published and how to locate it. Opinions are published in books called **reporters**, which gather together all of the opinions decided by a certain court or group of courts. There are many different reporters, and often the same opinion will appear in more than one. Supreme Court opinions are published in the *United States Reports,* abbreviated in citations as "U.S.," and in a few others. Federal appeals court opinions appear in the *Federal Reporter,* now in its third series, abbreviated "F.3d." The numbers in a citation refer to the volume of the reporter and the first page on which the opinion appears. The letters are the abbreviation of the reporter name. The order in which these letters and numbers appear is important: [Volume Number] [Abbreviation of Reporter Name] [First Page Number]. (For more on citing legal sources, see Chapter 6.)

So, for *Lawrence,* the citation looks like this: 539 U.S. 558.

If you go to a law library to the section that holds the *United States Reports,* you can pull volume 539 off of the shelf and flip to page 558, and on that page will be the first page of the *Lawrence* opinion.

## Hint: Docket Numbers

Cases are given another number as well, called the **docket number**, a number assigned by a court to identify a case. The docket number for *Lawrence* is 02–102, which refers to 2002 (the year the court heard the case) and the number that case falls in the term—the 102nd case. Although some student writing handbooks suggest using the docket number when you write a bibliographic entry for a case, legal professionals and scholars rarely uses docket numbers when citing cases. This is because there are other legal documents that the docket number refers to besides the main opinion, such as interim decisions on small legal questions. If you search the docket number for *Lawrence,* five documents appear. Thus, docket numbers are an imprecise way to refer to a judicial opinion, and lawyers are very concerned with precision. (More on docket numbers and citing cases appears in Chapter 6.)

In your case brief, then, you should write the abbreviated full name of the case, the citation of the case, and then the year the case was decided in parentheses. The case name and citation for a brief of *Lawrence* would look like this:

**Lawrence v. Texas, 539 U.S. 558 (2003)**

## Issue

The **issue** is the most important part of your brief; if you misunderstand the issue, you will misunderstand the entire case. The issue, sometimes called the *question presented*, is a statement of the legal question that the court must decide in the opinion. You can think of the issue as the "thesis statement" of the opinion. For these reasons, you should put the issue first in your case brief.

A court sometimes states directly what the issue is, using key phrases like these:

- "The issue presented in this case is whether . . ."
- "Today we must decide whether . . ."
- "The question presented to the court is whether . . ."

All of these key phrases contain the word "whether." When you are locating the issue, you should "look for the whether." The Supreme Court in *Lawrence* provides two statements of the issue. The second paragraph of the opinion, on page 562, begins this way: "The question before the Court is the validity of a Texas statute making it a crime for two persons of the same sex to engage in certain intimate sexual conduct." After providing the facts of the case, the court restates the issue on page 564, writing that "the case should be resolved by determining whether the petitioners were free as adults to engage in the private conduct in the exercise of their liberty under the due process clause of the Fourteenth Amendment of the Constitution." In the first issue statement, the court uses the key word "question." In the second, the court uses the key word "whether."

As you study cases, you will see that the way the court phrases the question often determines the answer. In other words, how the court frames the issue rhetorically sometimes predicts the outcome of the case.

You have experienced this sort of rhetorical framing in your daily life. For example, say your friend owns a Ferrari. You want to take it out on Saturday night because last week you totaled your car in an accident after you ran a red light. You ask your friend if you may borrow the car, and she responds with a question: "You don't think that I'm going to let you use my car after you trashed yours last week, do you?" There is really only one valid answer to this question—*No*. The way your friend asks the question tells you what her answer is going to be. When a question's phrasing implies its answer, we call it a **rhetorical question**. In

*Lawrence*, the way the majority frames the question tells you what the answer will be. Few Americans would disagree that "adults" are "free" to "engage in private conduct."

In your case brief, it is important that you accurately identify the legal issue at stake in the case. You need to write the issue in words that clearly identify the conflict, ideally *as a question that can be answered with a yes or no*. Issue questions in case briefs usually start with the word *does* rather than the word *whether*. Framing the issue as a yes/no question helps clarify the legal question and the holding of the case.

If you are writing a brief of a U.S. Supreme Court case, the issue question often fits this template: *Does [a law or statute] violate [a certain part of] the U.S. Constitution?* The Supreme Court is often asked to declare the constitutionality of a law or statute, that is, to compare a state or federal law to the Constitution and see if they agree. If they disagree, the Constitution wins—it *always* wins—and the state or federal law is declared unconstitutional. Issue questions for lower federal court and state court opinions can take many different forms, and you will learn to write these issue questions as you practice writing case briefs.

For the Supreme Court opinion in *Lawrence*, the issue question looks like the template:

> **Issue:** Does the Texas crime-against-nature statute violate the due process clause of the Fourteenth Amendment to the U.S. Constitution?

## Facts

New case briefers often put far too many facts in their case briefs. Remember this rule: You should only include *relevant facts* in your brief. What makes a fact relevant? Relevant facts have a direct impact on the outcome of a particular case. After you draft your facts section, try to shorten it as much as possible. Assess the relevance of each fact separately. Ask yourself whether the court's opinion would change if a particular fact were changed. If the answer is "no," then the fact is not relevant to the outcome of the case.

You should put the procedural history of a case in the facts section as well. Provide enough procedural history to explain how the case originated and how it ended up in the court whose opinion you are reading.

In *Lawrence*, it is not relevant that the men were named Lawrence and Garner, or that they lived outside of Houston (rather than another part of Texas), or that Lawrence was older than Garner. The relevant facts in *Lawrence* would be these:

> **Facts:** Defendants, two men, were arrested in their home for having sex in violation of the Texas crime-against-nature statute. The statute forbids "deviate sexual intercourse" between people of the same sex. The defendants were convicted and fined. They appealed their arrest and conviction through the Texas courts. The U.S. Supreme Court granted their petition for appeal.

## Holding

The holding, sometimes called the *ruling*, is the actual legal decision made by the court. In an opinion, the holding is often preceded by these key phrases: "We hold that . . ." or "We rule that. . . ." In order to make the legal issue and holding as clear as possible, you should phrase the holding as a short answer to the question you wrote in your issue. When you write the holding, you should start with the word "Yes" or "No," followed by a comma, and then a full statement of the holding. In a brief of *Lawrence*, the holding looks like this:

> **Holding:** Yes, the Texas crime-against-nature statute violates the due process clause of the Fourteenth Amendment to the U.S. Constitution.

## Reasoning

The reasoning section is the second-most-important part of a case brief, after the issue. In fact, if you count the words, the reasoning section should compose roughly half of your entire brief. If you finish your brief and your reasoning section seems short, review the judicial opinion to be sure you have addressed all of the arguments given by the court to support its ruling.

In the reasoning section, you go through the court's arguments one by one. You might find the **legal *topoi*** useful in conducting this analysis. The *topoi* are a list of the types of arguments that judges use in their opinions, presented in detail later in this chapter. Does the court rely on precedent—the prior rulings by the court? Does the court rely on scientific data or studies? Does the court appeal to morality or ethics?

After you have listed all of the arguments used by the court, examine each one more closely. Which arguments do you find more persuasive? Which are less persuasive? Why? Write your assessment of the arguments.

Remember, stating whether you agree or disagree with the court is *not* an adequate analysis of the court's arguments. You must also (1) identify the arguments used by the court and (2) assess whether the arguments are persuasive or not. Use the analytical tools you learned from rhetorical analysis. (See Chapter 1 for more on rhetorical analysis.)

The reasoning section of a brief of the *Lawrence* majority opinion excerpted in Chapter One might look like this:

**Reasoning:** The majority relies on precedent composed of due process right to privacy cases. They start with *Griswold v. CT*, then *Eisenstadt v. Baird*, and then *Roe v. Wade*. They then use this precedent and the facts of the current case to overturn *Bowers v. Hardwick*, a 1986 case that upheld a similar sodomy law in Georgia. The Court's reliance on *Roe* seems less persuasive than the other cases it uses because *Roe* stands on shaky ground today.

The Court makes ethical arguments when it argues that homosexuals, like heterosexuals, should have a right to private sexual relationships. However, this moral argument would be stronger if they addressed the competing moral claims in this case—the right to love and have relationships on one hand versus the "traditional" morals that many Americans believe in on the other hand.

The Court addresses historical arguments when it claims that "there is no longstanding history" of laws targeting homosexuals on page 568. They argue that laws forbidding sodomy were directed at heterosexual couples as well, and that it was not until the 1970s that laws targeting homosexuals first appeared. With this argument they seek to debunk the argument in *Bowers* that sodomy laws are deeply rooted in U.S. history. Their separation of sodomy laws from laws targeting homosexuals is accurate but feels unpersuasive. The fact is, like slavery and sexism, sodomy laws have indeed been around for a long time. They did not have to debunk the historical argument in order to declare them unconstitutional.

*(Continued)*

The Court brings in international law when it examines the European court's rulings on sodomy laws on page 576. The strong stance that Europe has taken against homophobic laws is persuasive to the extent that we care about what our peer nations are doing. Some judges care (like Kennedy) and some do not (like Scalia).

## Dissenting and Concurring Opinions

Many opinions, like *Lawrence*, contain more than one opinion. Sometimes, when judges fail to agree on the outcome of a case, the judges in the minority write a **dissenting opinion**, sometimes called a *dissent*. These opinions do not have the force of law, but they are important in other ways. Dissents give voice to a legal perspective that differs from that of the majority, a perspective that might be held by many Americans. Sometimes dissenting opinions are used years later when the Court overturns an earlier decision.

Occasionally, a justice will agree with the holding of a majority opinion but wishes to clarify a point of law. In this situation, the justice will write a **concurring opinion**, sometimes called a *concurrence*. For example, in *Lawrence*, Justice Sandra Day O'Connor wrote a concurring opinion. O'Connor agreed with the majority that the Texas statute was unconstitutional. She just disagreed as to how.

In your case brief, you should mention whether there are dissenting or concurring opinions and write short summaries of them. Point out the main arguments made by these secondary opinions, and note how they differ from the majority opinion.

In Chapter 1, you read an excerpt of O'Connor's concurrence and Scalia's dissent in *Lawrence*. Your brief must therefore discuss these two opinions:

**Concurrence:** O'Connor agrees that the Texas statute is unconstitutional but disagrees that it violates due process. She argues that because the statute targets homosexuals specifically, it violates equal protection. She also believes that *Bowers* should not be overturned.

**Dissent:** Scalia argues that legislatures should be allowed to make laws based on morals. He also argues that *Bowers* should not have been overturned because overturning the case creates inconsistency in the Court's rulings.

# LEGAL TOPOI

Legal *topoi* are categories of common arguments employed by judges, legal scholars, and lawyers. Writing the reasoning section and the dissenting and concurring summaries in your briefs becomes a lot easier when you understand the legal *topoi*, for they provide an analytical framework to organize the reasoning of a judicial opinion.

"*Topoi*" is a word used by ancient Greek rhetoricians that roughly translates as "topics" or "commonplaces." This section outlines seven *topoi* useful for analyzing judicial opinions and for generating legal arguments in your writing. There are more than seven types of arguments made by lawyers and judges, of course; this book provides the ones that are used most often. Nearly all arguments used by the Supreme Court to support its holding in *Lawrence* can be classified under one of the following *topoi*:

- Precedent
- Legislation
- History
- International or comparative law
- Morality
- Public policy
- Science

The legal *topoi* are useful for writing case briefs because they provide organization for the reasoning section of a brief. They are also useful for inventing arguments to support a thesis in a research paper. For this reason, we will return to the *topoi* in later chapters.

In the following, each *topos* (the singular of *topoi*) is presented with ideas for how judges, lawyers, and legal scholars use these arguments and for how to spot them in your reading of judicial opinions. As you become more familiar with the *topoi*, you will start to use them in your writing about law. You will also see that the *topoi* often overlap conceptually; it is good to notice how they relate to one another.

## Precedent

In the **Anglo-American legal system**, when judges make decisions or when lawyers make arguments, they turn to precedent for guidance first. The precedent of a particular case comprises all of the court opinions that have been decided on similar issues. This is judge-made law, which comes from the opinions that judges have made in earlier, similar cases. The guiding principle of precedent is that *like cases should be decided alike*.

However, lawyers often disagree about which cases are "like" the case at hand. For any given case, there are often many different lines of precedent to choose from, each yielding a different outcome. The lawyers for each side will argue that certain prior cases should be applied to the present case and certain cases should not, in order to gain a positive outcome for their clients.

To **analogize** (or *draw an analogy*), then, means to argue that an earlier case is similar to the case at hand, and therefore the case at hand should have the same outcome as the earlier case. To **distinguish** (or *draw a distinction*) means to point out differences between an earlier case and a case at hand and to argue that the earlier case should *not* affect the present case's outcome. This process of analogy and distinction is best illustrated by an example.

Let us say that a landlord and a tenant are disputing whether the landlord must pay to replace the tenant's belongings after a house fire. Poor wiring caused the fire, but neither the landlord nor the tenant knew the wiring was dangerous. In their arguments to the judge, the lawyers look to earlier cases that have facts similar to the present case—to the *precedent* for the present case. The lawyer for the tenant will argue that the damage caused by poor wiring is similar to an earlier case in which damage was caused by faulty pipes. In the earlier case, the landlord was required to pay for the damage. In order to make the argument that the cases are similar, lawyer analogizes the pipes in the earlier case with the wiring in the present case. The lawyer then concludes that since the landlord had to pay in the earlier case, the landlord in the present case should have to pay now.

On the contrary, the lawyer for the landlord will argue that the faulty-pipes case does not apply to this case because in the pipes case, the tenant warned the landlord that the pipes were leaking and the landlord refused to repair them. Thus, the earlier case is different from the present case because the landlord had knowledge of the problem and chose to ignore it. In making this argument, the lawyer distinguishes the earlier case from the present case. The judge has to decide whether the similarity between pipes and wires is more persuasive than the difference between the cases—that the landlord received warning.

The lesson to learn from this example is that there is no perfect precedent—no case is *exactly* like one that came before. It is a lawyer's job to analogize and distinguish cases on behalf of a client's position.

Even if an earlier case is similar to the case at hand, only certain court opinions can operate as precedent. In order for an earlier opinion to be precedent in a present case, the opinion must have been given by the same court now hearing a case or by a court with even greater power. For example, the U.S. Supreme Court has power over all civilian courts in the United States, both state and federal. Lower courts must follow Supreme Court opinions, and only the Supreme Court can **overturn** its own earlier opinions and declare them incorrect. It will do so for a variety of reasons, but only rarely. In *Lawrence*, the Supreme Court overturned its earlier decision in *Bowers v. Hardwick*. A decision made by the same court or a more powerful court in the **path of appeal** is called **controlling precedent** because the earlier decision controls the decisions that come later. Courts are required to follow controlling precedent.

Sometimes a court will choose to follow a ruling of a court of similar or lesser power because it finds that court's rulings to be persuasive. The earlier decision is not controlling but it is too important to be ignored completely. For example, the North Carolina Supreme Court might follow a ruling of the South Carolina Supreme Court, a court with no legal power in North Carolina, because the decision is persuasive. In summary, a court may choose to follow **persuasive precedent**, but it is not required to.

Applying the precedent *topos* to *Lawrence*, we see that the U.S. Supreme Court turned to *Roe v. Wade*, *Griswold v. Connecticut*, and other due process cases dealing with the right to privacy in order to justify its decision to overturn *Bowers* and strike down the Texas statute.

## Legislation

Another major source of law in our legal system is **legislation**, or laws made by any representative body or legislature. Legislation comprises laws made by the U.S. Congress, by state legislatures, or by local governments in towns and cities. The U.S. Constitution falls under the legislation *topos* as well, and it is the most powerful legislation in the United States. When judges and lawyers use legislation in their arguments, they often argue for a particular interpretation of a statute. They will give many reasons for why a statute should be interpreted a certain way. They might argue for an interpretation because it is supported by the **plain meaning** of the statute, that is, by the statute's language read in an ordinary way. They might argue that the **legislative intent** dictates such an interpretation and examine the various documents produced by the legislature to try to uncover their intent.

In *Lawrence*, the U.S. Supreme Court stuck for the most part to the plain meaning of the Texas statute rather than study the intent of the Texas legislature. In fact, in *Lawrence*, there does not seem to be much debate over what the statute meant, only whether this meaning violated the Constitution. Based on the Texas statute's criminalization of homosexual sodomy, the Supreme Court declared the statute unconstitutional.

## History

If the precedent *topos* examines the legal history of a case, the history *topos* examines the nonlegal history of a case—the way our society has acted under similar circumstances in the past. Historical study helps courts figure out how we should act today. Courts will turn to history to justify a ruling, arguing that the ruling aligns with our society's valued historical practices and is therefore valid. Other times courts will use history to justify a *change* in the law because a certain historical event or law seems wrong to our modern eyes. The court then chooses to correct this historical injustice with its ruling.

Be on the lookout for both types of arguments made with the history *topos*—the ones that align with history, as well as the ones that seek to fix historical injustices.

In *Lawrence*, the justices of the majority argue that the history of the United States does not support discrimination against homosexuals and argue that it was not until the 1970s that states began to write discrimination against homosexuals into their laws.

## International or Comparative Law

The U.S. Supreme Court uses the international or comparative law *topos* when it turns to the laws of our peer nations to help decide what the law should be in our country. In cases such as these, the Supreme Court compares our laws with those of other nations. State courts use the comparative law *topos* as well when they examine what their sister states have ruled. Implicit in the *topos* of international or comparative law is the idea that only our "peer" nations or "sister" states will guide us. Of course, which countries and states count as our "peers" is subject to argument. Usually, the courts turn to countries whose histories and societal values align with ours, such as Canada or the countries of Western Europe. State courts usually turn to the laws of nearby states rather than those in different regions of the country, or to states with similar political leanings.

International law also comes into play when courts discuss the reputation of the U.S. in other countries. For example, our international standing was very important in the *Brown v. Board of Education* decision because other countries were highly critical of racial segregation in the United States. At the time, the former USSR—our Cold War adversary—used American racial segregation to argue that communism is a better form of government than capitalism. Our international standing thus influenced the court's decision to end racial segregation in schools and other public places.

In the *Lawrence* majority opinion, Justice Kennedy suggests that our laws should fall into step with those of our peer nations in Western Europe, which have decriminalized homosexual acts. He lists opinions of European courts to support this position.

## Morality

New legal writers are often confused by the morality *topos*, arguing that judges should keep their "personal morality" out of court opinions. Morality is rarely "personal," however. Rather, **morals** are community-driven rules created by a group of people to govern their collective behavior. In many ways, morals look a lot like laws.

Thus, the morality *topos* examines the shared morals of a community in order to determine what laws should be. The morality *topos* is often closely tied with the history *topos*, as community morals develop over time and are often rooted in the community's history.

In his dissenting opinion in *Lawrence*, Justice Scalia invokes the morality *topos*. He argues that states should be allowed to create laws based on their shared morals and that the federal courts should not interfere with these laws. Scalia actually uses the word "moral," which should clue you into his use of this *topos*.

Courts make morality arguments in subtle ways as well. Often, these arguments use words such as "must," "should," or something similar to imply a proper course of behavior. The majority in *Lawrence* makes a subtle morality argument when they write, "The petitioners are entitled to respect for their private lives." The word "entitled" implies that the source of this entitlement is not law (since Lawrence and Garner's sexual relationship was illegal), but rather a moral code with which the statute conflicts. They invoked this code whenever they wrote "liberty." Thus, in *Lawrence*, two sets of morals come into conflict: personal liberty and more "traditional," or historical, sexual values.

## Public Policy

Simply put, **public policy** is composed of the decisions a government makes regarding certain conflicts and the effects these decisions have on the public. The public policy *topos* helps us determine what the consequences of a law will be and whether these consequences will help or hurt society as a whole. A lawyer uses the public policy *topos* when he or she argues that a law should be changed because following it will have harmful ramifications for a large group of people. When a judicial opinion discusses "consequences," "results," "implications," or similar concepts, it invokes the public policy *topos*.

Justice Scalia makes a public policy argument in his *Lawrence* dissent when he suggests that allowing sodomy will have negative consequences. If sodomy is legal, Scalia argues, then our rule "treat like cases alike" dictates that prostitution, incest, and bestiality must be legal as well, and, he argues, allowing these practices will be harmful to our public health and safety.

## Science

Sometimes laws are written or changed based on the findings of scientific or statistical studies. Whenever a court turns to data gathered by researchers rather than by lawyers they employ the science *topos*. Look for phrases such as "studies show" or "evidence suggests" to find instances of the science *topos*. For example, in overturning school segregation in *Brown v. Board of Education*, the Supreme Court relied on psychological studies revealing the harmful effects of segregation on children.

## WRITING A CASE BRIEF

Remember, a case brief is a tool: It creates a manageable outline of the important parts of a judicial opinion and helps you understand an opinion's complex parts. Generally, a case brief should use subheadings in bold or capital letters to aid in quick retrieval of information. If your teacher assigns a written case brief for your class, use the following suggestions and checklist to be sure you have followed the format correctly.

## Read the Case Twice

Read the case you are to brief two times. The first time, you should annotate the text with the parts of a brief—underline and label the issue, the description of the facts of the case, the holding, and so on. The second time you read, write your case brief as you go.

## Frame the Issue as a Yes/No Question

Your issue statement should start with "Did" or "Does," not "Whether." It should end with a question mark. The holding should *answer* this question with a declarative sentence that begins with a "yes" or "no." Reframing the issue as a question and putting it into your words helps you better understand the issue of a case.

## Relevant Facts Only

Beginning brief writers put too many facts in their briefs. Remember: Only include *relevant* facts in your brief, the facts that have a direct impact on the outcome of the case.

## Reasoning Section Should Be Half

The reasoning section is the most important part of your brief and should be at least half of the total length. You should use the legal *topoi* to organize this section, discussing each of the *topoi* that the court invokes in its reasoning. Complete sentences are not necessary in the reasoning section—it should contain short summary statements only. You should also *assess* the strengths and weaknesses of each reason, pointing out rhetorical fallacies if you find them.

### Case Brief Checklist

- Case name and citation: Did you use the abbreviated full case name? Is the title italicized? Have you written the citation properly? Did you include the year?

- Issue: Do you frame your issue as a question? Does the issue tell what the case is about in one sentence? Can the question be answered with a yes or no?

- Facts: Is every fact you selected relevant to the outcome of the case? Did you include a brief summary of the procedural history?

- Holding: Do you begin your statement of the holding with a "yes" or "no"? Does the holding answer the question posed in the issue?

- Reasoning: Do you address all of the arguments that the court gives for its holding? Did you use the legal *topoi* to organize the arguments? Do you evaluate the persuasiveness of these arguments?

- Dissent/concurrence: Is there a concurrence or dissent in this case? Do you provide an adequate summary and analysis of these opinions?

# 3

## ANATOMY OF LEGAL SCHOLARSHIP

As we learned in Chapter 1, we can think of legal writing as composed of two separate but related activities: professional legal writing and scholarly legal writing. These two types of legal writing are defined by the genres they produce. Professional legal writers produce contracts, briefs, wills, and other professional documents. Scholarly legal writers produce academic legal documents such as law journal articles, book reviews, and case notes. This chapter focuses on scholarly legal writing, approaching legal scholarship as a process that can be studied as separate stages. When this book refers to "legal writing" or "legal writers" in this chapter, however, it refers to *all* legal writers, both professional and scholarly.

The line between professional legal writing and scholarly legal writing is a fine one, however, and many legal writers participate in both legal writing communities. Legal scholars study the practice of law in their articles; practicing lawyers turn to law journal articles for guidance on new areas of law. In fact, legal scholarship serves an important function for the development of law in the United States. Law journal articles typically examine areas of law that are uncertain or contentious and make suggestions for how to improve these areas. Lawyers and judges use legal scholarship when making arguments and decisions in these uncertain areas. Lawyers cite legal scholarship in memos and briefs; judges cite it in their orders and opinions. In this way, legal scholarship is central to legal practice. As our society changes, law must change. For example, new technologies, such as the Internet and cellular phones, require new laws to govern them. Legal scholarship pioneers these changes.

In this chapter we examine three different organizational frameworks: classical oration, professional legal writing, and scholarly legal writing. The chapter also guides you through the selection of a topic and development of a thesis for legal scholarship. You will learn how to support a thesis with evidence and the types of sources you will use. Lastly, you will learn how to write a special type of outline that is particularly useful in writing about law, one that pairs the arguments you make in your writing with the sources that support those arguments.

To begin, let us return to the definition of legal writing given in Chapter 1: Legal writing is *the skill of making legal claims and supporting them with authority.* Legal scholarship, like all legal writing, is driven by **authority**, that is, primary and secondary sources and other types of evidence used to support legal arguments. Every claim that a legal writer makes is supported by evidence: a case, a statute, a law journal article, or some other legal or even nonlegal source. Starting now, you must begin to think of arguments and authority as a joined pair. If you make a claim, you must support it.

Keep in mind the following essential characteristics of strong legal writing. First, legal writers integrate research, rhetoric, and argumentation into one text. Legal writers use court opinions and other primary legal documents as sources. They also effectively use secondary sources and place themselves in a dialogue with these sources. Legal writers strike an appropriate tone for their audiences, a tone driven by evidence rather than by emotion, even when the subject matter evokes strong feelings. Legal writers avoid dramatic language and hyperbole, striving instead to move the audience with weight of evidence and strength of research. Lastly, legal writing is *extremely* well organized. On this note, let us study some organizational frameworks that aid organization.

## ORGANIZATIONAL FRAMEWORKS

Ancient Greek and Roman rhetoricians helped create modern legal argumentation. They developed an arrangement, or framework, for making legal arguments, a framework so successful that speakers eventually used it for all sorts of rhetorical situations. This framework is still with us in a variety of forms, including the organization of professional legal documents, the paradigms of legal analysis taught in law schools, and the structure of scholarly writing, both in the legal field and in other academic areas. The word "framework" might sound prescriptive, like a strict structure that limits creativity. Instead, try to think of frameworks in terms of their rhetorical purpose: to make complicated arguments easier for particular audiences to understand and use.

Certain organizational frameworks complement certain genres of documents. As we learned in Chapter 1, genres are types of texts designed to accomplish certain purposes and therefore share conventions. For example, a research article is a genre designed to create new knowledge in a certain field, a field such as law.

Law journal articles share conventions such as titles, thesis statements, citation of sources in Bluebook format, the use of paragraphs, introductions and conclusions, and so on.

How the author arranges arguments, background material, and evidence within a particular genre depends on the organizational framework the author uses. Certain genres favor certain frameworks, but there are many of these frameworks available. Remember: Frameworks are tools for sorting through information and arguments and putting them into order in a way that will be most persuasive to your audience. You should always keep your audience in mind when organizing your material.

This chapter presents three different frameworks:

- *Classical Framework:* The framework of classical oratory, developed by Greek and Roman rhetoricians.
- *C-RAC (Conclusion, Rule, Application, Conclusion):* The argumentation framework of professional legal writing. It was developed with the audience of busy legal professionals in mind.
- *Scholarly Framework:* A framework developed by drawing on the best of the classical and C-RAC frameworks often used by legal scholars. This is the framework we will rely upon for the rest of this book.

## Classical Framework

Classical rhetoricians of Greece, and later of Rome, created a framework for oratory that is still used today. Roman rhetoricians Cicero and Quintilian helped solidify this framework, which was originally designed for making legal arguments. Over decades and centuries, rhetoricians of all kinds, not just those who argued about law, adopted the framework. You might find this framework useful if you need to prepare an oral presentation, as it was originally designed for speeches. Originally, this framework had six parts:

- Exordium
- Narration
- Partition

- Confirmation
- Refutation
- Peroration

Let us use this framework to examine one of the founding documents of the United States—the Declaration of Independence. Here is an excerpt of the document.

## The Declaration of Independence

*Authored by Thomas Jefferson, 1776*

When in the Course of human events it becomes necessary for one people to dissolve the political bands which have connected them with another and to assume among the powers of the earth, the separate and equal station to which the Laws of Nature and of Nature's God entitle them, a decent respect to the opinions of mankind requires that they should declare the causes which impel them to the separation.

We hold these truths to be self-evident, that all men are created equal, that they are endowed by their Creator with certain unalienable Rights, that among these are Life, Liberty and the pursuit of Happiness.—That to secure these rights, Governments are instituted among Men, deriving their just powers from the consent of the governed,—That whenever any Form of Government becomes destructive of these ends, it is the Right of the People to alter or to abolish it, and to institute new Government, laying its foundation on such principles and organizing its powers in such form, as to them shall seem most likely to effect their Safety and Happiness. Prudence, indeed, will dictate that Governments long established should not be changed for light and transient causes; and accordingly all experience hath shewn that mankind are more disposed to suffer, while evils are sufferable than to right themselves by abolishing the forms to which they are accustomed. But when a long train of abuses and usurpations, pursuing invariably the same Object evinces a design to reduce them under absolute Despotism, it is their right, it is their duty, to throw off such Government, and to provide new Guards for their future security.—Such has been the patient sufferance of these Colonies;

*(Continued)*

and such is now the necessity which constrains them to alter their former Systems of Government. The history of the present King of Great Britain is a history of repeated injuries and usurpations, all having in direct object the establishment of an absolute Tyranny over these States. To prove this, let Facts be submitted to a candid world.

He has refused his Assent to Laws, the most wholesome and necessary for the public good.

He has forbidden his Governors to pass Laws of immediate and pressing importance, unless suspended in their operation till his Assent should be obtained; and when so suspended, he has utterly neglected to attend to them.

He has refused to pass other Laws for the accommodation of large districts of people, unless those people would relinquish the right of Representation in the Legislature, a right inestimable to them and formidable to tyrants only.

He has called together legislative bodies at places unusual, uncomfortable, and distant from the depository of their Public Records, for the sole purpose of fatiguing them into compliance with his measures.

He has dissolved Representative Houses repeatedly, for opposing with manly firmness his invasions on the rights of the people. . . .

We, therefore, the Representatives of the united States of America, in General Congress, Assembled, appealing to the Supreme Judge of the world for the rectitude of our intentions, do, in the Name, and by Authority of the good People of these Colonies, solemnly publish and declare, That these united Colonies are, and of Right ought to be Free and Independent States, that they are Absolved from all Allegiance to the British Crown, and that all political connection between them and the State of Great Britain, is and ought to be totally dissolved; and that as Free and Independent States, they have full Power to levy War, conclude Peace, contract Alliances, establish Commerce, and to do all other Acts and Things which Independent States may of right do.—And for the support of this Declaration, with a firm reliance on the protection of Divine Providence, we mutually pledge to each other our Lives, our Fortunes, and our sacred Honor.

**Exordium**   The **exordium** of classical rhetoric resembles the introductions of today's spoken and written frameworks—like the introduction of the five-paragraph essay you might have written in high school. The exordium introduces the main issue under argument, taking into account how familiar the audience would be with the topic. It also puts the audience into a receptive frame of mind to hear the speech, softening up a hostile audience or firing up a friendly one. In the Declaration of Independence, the first paragraph functions as an exordium:

> When in the Course of human events it becomes necessary for one people to dissolve the political bands which have connected them with another and to assume among the powers of the earth, the separate and equal station to which the Laws of Nature and of Nature's God entitle them, a decent respect to the opinions of mankind requires that they should declare the causes which impel them to the separation.

This paragraph states the purpose of the document—"to dissolve the political bands" between the colonies and England. It creates sympathy for the speakers' position by declaring that the colonists are not acting unlawfully; rather, they are entitled to the "separate and equal station to which the Laws of Nature and of Nature's God entitle them." It creates a tone of modesty by stating that the writers have "a decent respect to the opinions of mankind" and are listing grievances merely because of this respect, not out of a desire to complain.

**Narration**   The **narration** (*narratio* in Latin) presents background information on issue at hand, what we might call the *backstory*. This is the information the audience would need to know in order to make an informed decision about the issue. Like all aspects of this framework, the narration is audience driven. If your audience is familiar with the subject matter, you need to provide less information in the narration; if your audience is unfamiliar, you need to provide more.

In the Declaration, most of the second paragraph is a narration, providing the philosophical underpinnings of the document's arguments:

We hold these truths to be self-evident, that all men are created equal, that they are endowed by their Creator with certain unalienable Rights, that among these are Life, Liberty and the pursuit of Happiness.—That to secure these rights, Governments are instituted among Men, deriving their just powers from the consent of the governed,. . . . But when a long train of abuses and usurpations, pursuing invariably the same Object evinces a design to reduce them under absolute Despotism, it is their right, it is their duty, to throw off such Government, and to provide new Guards for their future security. Such has been the patient sufferance of these Colonies; and such is now the necessity which constrains them to alter their former Systems of Government.

In 1776, the notion that "all men are created equal" was anything but "self-evident." This was an age of deep class divisions, monarchies, and slavery. To most readers, the rights to "Life, Liberty, and the pursuit of Happiness" would not have seemed "inalienable." The various audiences of this document—King George III of England, the citizens of England and of France, and the American colonists—would have needed this background information to understand the arguments of the Declaration.

This section also connects this philosophy to the particular history of the colonies and their relationship to England. This backstory leads the reader to the present moment in which independence is declared.

**Partition**    The **partition** (*partitio* in Latin) of the classical rhetorical framework divides the main issue into smaller, manageable parts and tells the audience the order in which the speaker will address each part. The partition is like the table of contents of a book or "roadmap" of a speech. (See Chapter 8 for more on roadmaps.)

The history of the present King of Great Britain is a history of repeated injuries and usurpations, all having in direct object the establishment of an absolute Tyranny over these States. To prove this, let Facts be submitted to a candid world.

Here, the authors of the Declaration provide what we would call a "thesis statement"—the "absolute Tyranny" England has established over the colonies, forcing the colonies to rebel. After this thesis, the authors tell us that they will provide a list of "Facts" to support their position. What follows is a detailed list of grievances against the King.

**Confirmation**    The **confirmation** (*confirmatio* in Latin) is composed of arguments that support the main argument and examples and evidence that prove these supporting arguments. This section is the "meat" of the speech or text, the moment when the speaker gives each part of the argument and supports each part with authority. In the Declaration, the list of grievances composes the confirmation of the document.

> He has refused his Assent to Laws, the most wholesome and necessary for the public good.
>
> He has forbidden his Governors to pass Laws of immediate and pressing importance, unless suspended in their operation till his Assent should be obtained; and when so suspended, he has utterly neglected to attend to them.
>
> He has refused to pass other Laws for the accommodation of large districts of people, unless those people would relinquish the right of Representation in the Legislature, a right inestimable to them and formidable to tyrants only.

This is merely a brief excerpt of a very long list of complaints the colonists lodged against the King of England. The list is so long, in fact, and uses such repetitive sentence structure that it gains a poetic, almost hypnotic quality as it is read. The authors hoped to persuade, in part, by the sheer volume of evidence.

**Refutation**    The **refutation** (*refutatio* in Latin) presents possible objections that an audience member might have to the argument the speaker makes. These objections are often called **counterarguments**. After presenting the counterarguments, the speaker presents rebuttals, or what we might think of as "counter-counterarguments." The rhetorical work of counterargument and rebuttal strengthens the overall argument because the audience knows that the speaker has considered possible weaknesses and refuted them. The Declaration does not use this technique; however, Sojourner Truth's speech, presented later in this chapter, provides an excellent example of the strategy of refutation.

**Peroration**    The **peroration** (*peroratio* in Latin) brings all of the arguments, supporting arguments, and counterarguments together into a neat finish. It is the conclusion of the speech or text. Here the speaker might advise a course of action based on the arguments provided in the confirmation.

The Declaration has a grand peroration in which the authors declare their separation from England and their intention to wage war to support this declaration. They invoke "the Supreme Judge of the world" and "Divine Providence" for protection.

> We, therefore, the Representatives of the united States of America, in General Congress, Assembled, appealing to the Supreme Judge of the world for the rectitude of our intentions, do, in the Name, and by Authority of the good People of these Colonies, solemnly publish and declare, That these united Colonies are, and of Right ought to be Free and Independent States, that they are Absolved from all Allegiance to the British Crown, and that all political connection between them and the State of Great Britain, is and ought to be totally dissolved; and that as Free and Independent States, they have full Power to levy War, conclude Peace, contract Alliances, establish Commerce, and to do all other Acts and Things which Independent States may of right do.—And for the support of this Declaration, with a firm reliance on the protection of Divine Providence, we mutually pledge to each other our Lives, our Fortunes, and our sacred Honor.

The classical framework is still used today—unchanged—by political speech writers, public speakers, authors of newspaper editorials, and many other contemporary rhetoricians. Over the centuries, the framework also led to the creation of new frameworks, designed for new rhetorical situations and new audiences. The legal framework described next is one of these highly particularized frameworks that has roots in the classical framework.

## C-RAC Framework

Most lawyers can think back to the early days of law school when they first encountered the acronym **C-RAC** or something similar. C-RAC (pronounced *see-rack*) refers to the basic framework of legal analysis, composed of four steps:

- Conclusion
- Rule
- Application
- Conclusion

Professional legal writing depends upon the C-RAC framework for its strong and predictable organization.

C-RAC is very strict and formulaic. It is highly predictable and leaves little room for creative structuring of professional legal documents. This predictive nature of legal documents has an important rhetorical purpose driven by the audience of these documents. Lawyers, judges, and other legal professionals are extremely busy people. They read professional legal documents in order to learn what the law is, to learn how to rule on an issue, or to learn how to advise a client—but *not* to be entertained.

C-RAC arises in the context of a legal question, one that the legal writer needs to answer through research. Here are examples of legal questions that might be examined: "Is a landlord liable if a tree branch destroys the tenant's car?" "Is a defendant guilty of statutory rape when the victim lied about his age?" The legal writer must first research the laws that apply to each issue—the *rules* of the case. Then the legal writer *applies* these rules to the specific facts of the case at hand. After applying the rule to the facts, the legal writer can draw a *conclusion*.

This might be the order in which the writing occurs, but this is *not* the order in which the writing is presented to the audience. Instead, the *conclusion comes first*. An old maxim of legal writing goes like this: "First say what you are going to say, then say it, then say what you just said." This maxim correlates with the C-RAC framework: Conclusion (what you are going to say), rule and analysis (say it), conclusion (what you just said).

As you read about C-RAC, think about ways scholarly or academic writers can learn from the strictness of legal writing. Throughout this section, we will use the legal question on statutory rape just presented: "Is a defendant guilty of statutory rape when the victim lied about his age?"

**Conclusion**    The placement of the conclusion at the beginning of a document is the most striking quality of the C-RAC framework. Because they are in a hurry, the audiences of professional legal documents want the conclusions stated first. Cliffhangers, plot twists, and surprise endings have *no place* in professional legal writing. The statement of conclusion frames the rest of the legal analysis, giving readers a clear sense of purpose as they read on. They know *why* they are reading about a specific rule of law because they already know the endpoint of the argument.

Drawing from our example about statutory rape, the legal writer might write a conclusion stating that the defendant in this case is still guilty of statutory rape even though the victim claimed to be above the age of consent; statutory rape is a strict liability crime, which means that knowledge on the part of the defendant is not required for a finding of guilt.

**Rule**    The rule in the C-RAC framework is the law the writer applies in the case. The rule is hardly a given—sometimes the dispute in a case centers on which law applies in the first place. To find the rule, the legal writer searches through statutes, case law, and other sources of law to discover which relevant rules apply, then presents those rules in this section of the framework. (See Chapter 1 for a discussion of the sources of law.)

Returning to our example, the legal writer might present the criminal statute governing statutory rape in the jurisdiction in which the crime occurred. This statute might say that sex with any person, male or female, who is below the age of eighteen is statutory rape, regardless of whether the perpetrator had actual knowledge of the victim's age.

**Application**    The application section of the C-RAC framework is the heart of legal analysis. The rules and the facts come together to support the conclusion drawn by the legal writer. (If there are subarguments to an issue, each one needs to be analyzed separately.) Here, the legal writer would turn to case law to study how similar cases have been decided in the past and whether courts have interpreted a statute in a particular way. If the statute is particularly ambiguous or new, the legal writer might turn to legal scholarship for some elucidation of the issue.

The legal writer in our example would give the detailed facts of the case at hand, describing how the defendant met the victim shortly before the crime occurred and could not have known the victim's true age. Furthermore, when the defendant asked the victim how old he was, the victim lied and said he was nineteen years old. Lastly, the defendant admits to having sex with the victim. Given these facts, in light of the law of this jurisdiction, the defendant is guilty of statutory rape. All the prosecutor must prove is that sex with a minor occurred—not that the defendant *knew* that the victim was under the age of consent.

**Conclusion**    In the final part of this analytical framework, the legal writer presents the conclusions drawn from the rule and application.

Often, the writer will restate the conclusion from the opening section and add a statement describing some action that should be taken on the part of the reader in light of this conclusion. In our example, the legal writer might advise the defense attorney to seek a plea bargain on behalf of the defendant because the likelihood of winning at trial is slim.

Now that we have examined the frameworks of classical oratory and legal analysis, we will look at a third framework that brings together the strengths of these frameworks and the conventions of academic writing.

## Scholarly Framework

The last framework we will examine in this chapter is a scholarly framework that draws on the strengths of classical rhetoricians and of professional legal writers. You will find this framework useful in the early stages of a research process as you develop a thesis, supporting arguments, counterarguments, and rebuttals. This framework is designed not only for scholarly writing in general, but also for scholarly legal writing in particular, by taking into consideration the two main audiences who read this genre. Let us review these audiences.

First, scholarly legal writing is read by practicing lawyers and judges. Lawyers use scholarly articles to help make legal arguments in the courtroom and cite them in their briefs to judges and memos to other lawyers. Judges refer to them when crafting decisions about new areas of law and cite them in their opinions. This professional audience, as we know, is a very busy one. They need to know quickly if the article they are reading is useful for their purposes.

Second, scholarly legal writing is read by scholars—those who are conducting research in law and in other fields such as sociology, history, economics, and the many other areas of study that use legal research. These readers might be slightly less busy than legal professionals but still prefer to have a clear statement of your argument and conclusions at the beginning of an article.

What follows is a short summary of the elements of this framework. The rest of the chapter will elaborate on these elements.

**Thesis**    The thesis is the main point of an author's research stated in terms of an argument. (This section of the scholarly framework aligns with the conclusion of the C-RAC framework.) The scholarly thesis states clearly and succinctly the author's position, a conclusion based on the research the author has performed and that the author will prove throughout the text.

Some new writers are surprised to learn that even research papers have arguments, theses that writers strive to prove with supporting arguments and evidence. Law journal articles make all sorts of arguments, for example, about how the Constitution should be interpreted, about how to punish criminals, or about what should be protected as free speech.

Despite occasional similarities in topic, arguments in law journal articles are stated more subtly than the arguments you find on the editorial page of a newspaper. A law journal article on free speech has a different rhetorical purpose than an editorial on the same topic. Authors of a law journal articles know that legal professionals, including judges, expect to be guided by their work. They thus write in a tone of professional authority. The author of an editorial seeks to attract attention and persuade the general public. Therefore, an editorialist's tone will most likely be confrontational, emotional, and even sarcastic. Be aware of tone in crafting your thesis: The appropriate tone for legal writing (and most academic writing) is one of critical distance, not emotional hyperbole.

**Supporting Arguments**    In the partition section of the classical framework, the speaker or writer divides the main argument into more manageable parts. These parts are supporting arguments—arguments that support your thesis. Scholars use supporting arguments to divide and conquer a larger research project. The stronger supporting arguments you have, the stronger your thesis will be. You can use the legal *topoi* to generate supporting arguments or other brainstorming methods. Each supporting argument will need to be supported by authority found through research, otherwise known as evidence.

**Evidence**    Evidence is the fruit of research. It is the proof that scholars use to support their theses and supporting arguments. Think of supporting arguments as always paired with the evidence that supports them. Evidence can be found in a variety of places—statutes, case law, legal scholarship, scholarship and research of other fields besides law, personal experience, observations, and interviews.

**Counterarguments and Rebuttals**    Strong writers anticipate the counterarguments of readers who might disagree with their theses or supporting arguments and provide strong arguments to rebut them. This section of the scholarly framework aligns with the refutation of the classical framework. By anticipating the arguments of readers who might disagree and by providing strong rebuttals to the counterarguments, a writer appears to have carefully thought about all possibilities. This makes the writer's position stronger and more persuasive.

After you develop your thesis and supporting arguments, you should list all of the counterarguments to your position you can think of. Some students believe that giving the arguments for "the other side" will weaken their own arguments. This is not true. By listing each counterargument and providing a rebuttal, you have actually created even more supporting arguments for your thesis.

**Conclusion**    Conclusions are notoriously difficult to write. Drawing from the classical framework and from C-RAC, we can see that effective conclusions bring together the arguments and evidence presented in an article and reinforce the overall thesis. However, they do something else too: they advise. They make suggestions for actions that should be taken in light of the research presented in the article. Think about answering the question "Now what?" when you write your conclusion. Now that the reader has read your article, what should they do?

# CREATING AND SUPPORTING A THESIS

All arguments have a **thesis**, a main point of contention that can be summarized in a short sentence. In scholarly legal writing, a thesis is supported by smaller, supporting arguments paired with evidence. In a paper of ten to twenty pages, the thesis should be stated succinctly and with simple sentence structure, in one or two sentences, near the end of the introductory paragraph of your paper. (Chapter 5 discusses the organization of introductory paragraphs.)

Theses can take a variety of forms but are often signaled by a few commonly used phrases: "This article suggests that / argues that / contends that / proposes that . . ." or "I suggest that / argue that / contend that / propose that. . . ." Some theses are more strongly worded than others, depending on the writer's style as well as the persuasive tone the writer hopes to create.

The best way to learn about scholarly legal theses is to read scholarly legal writing. Conduct a search for law journal articles on a topic that interests you. (See Chapter 4 for guidance on searching articles using online databases.) Read the first few pages of each article and see if you can spot the thesis statement. On a piece of paper, write down the thesis statements of these articles. Compare them:

- What similarities do you find in the theses?
- Do you get a sense of their general construction?
- Are some more strongly worded than others?

- Do some sound weak and some sound strong? Why?
- Which style do you find more persuasive?

## Creating a Thesis

It is a maxim of rhetoric that *we do not argue about topics upon which there is agreement*. In other words, verifiable facts are not subject to argument, nor are topics upon which there is strong consensus.

A corollary of this statement holds that we do not argue about issues if an authority we respect has settled them. For example, although we may never know who "really" won the 2000 U.S. presidential election, at this point there are few who would argue that George W. Bush's presidency was unlawful. Once the Supreme Court gave its pronouncement in *Bush v. Gore* (2000), the dispute was settled—even though the election results were never fully verified.

In law, we would call the 2000 election dispute **moot**, which means the conflict has already been resolved or has somehow been placed beyond the practical reach of the law. To argue about *Bush v. Gore* now, especially since Bush is no longer in office, is purely an academic and theoretical exercise, with little practical significance. You run the risk of boring your readers because they will have a hard time staying interested in an insignificant argument. As a general rule, topics for scholarly legal writing should avoid mootness and insignificance.

Most scholarly theses begin as topics of interest to the writer. Through research, writers refine topics into theses. Let us study this process using an example.

In our example, the writer is interested in gun control. She will discover through research that the Supreme Court made an important ruling on handgun laws in *District of Columbia v. Heller* in 2008, declaring a Washington, D.C., handgun ban unconstitutional. The *Heller* case casts doubt on the legitimacy of all gun control laws in the United States. Now, to argue that *Heller* was decided correctly or incorrectly violates the maxim about mootness. However, our legal writer might do an examination of *Heller* in order to argue that all other handgun bans in the country must fall in light of the *Heller* ruling. That argument would have practical significance and deals with disputes that are far from settled.

You can mine your class readings and discussions to find places where the law is unsettled. Read recent Supreme Court cases in areas that interest you to see if new questions or ambiguities are created by these decisions. Blogs are a great source for discovering current controversy in law. Legal blogs—sometimes called "blawgs"—track these controversies. For example, the SCOTUSblog (**http://www.scotusblog.com**) follows recent developments in the Supreme Court. For a directory of legal blogs, see **http://www.blawg.com**.

## Supporting a Thesis

Once you have an idea of your main argument for your research, that is, once you have refined your topic into a thesis, you must begin to think of the ways you can support, or prove, your thesis. Like any big job, proving a thesis is often easier to do in smaller parts. Break your thesis into smaller, supporting arguments, which are easier to research and write about. Supporting arguments, then, are like minitheses.

One way you can develop supporting arguments is by using the legal *topoi* presented in Chapter 2. The *topoi* can help you brainstorm. Write your thesis at the top of a page. Then, list the *topoi* beneath the thesis, leaving a few lines between each one for jotting down ideas. Next, go through each of the *topoi*, thinking about the ways that each one relates to your thesis. Write down any possible connections you can think of.

Let us return to our legal writer who is interested in the future of gun control legislation in light of *Heller*. Under "precedent" she would write down *U.S. v. Miller* (1938), the last big ruling on gun control before *Heller*. She would also list any other major state court or federal appeals court decisions that deal with gun control. Under "legislation" she would note that there are many laws that seem to conflict with *Heller* and that she needs to research them. She would also write down the Second Amendment to the U.S. Constitution.

These notes do not look like arguments right now—they are simply places to start research, like minitopics. As you research, you refine them into arguments, and you will support those arguments with evidence.

## EVIDENCE

Evidence supports your supporting arguments and your thesis. Evidence, also called "authority" and "sources," can be scholarly sources, personal experience, scientific observations, statistics, interviews, and any other proof that you gather through your research. The more evidence you provide, the stronger your supporting arguments will be. As you will see later in this chapter, certain types of evidence are more authoritative than others. You need to be selective when choosing your evidence.

A basic rule for scholarly legal writing (and most academic writing generally) is that *you should never present a supporting argument in your paper without evidence to support it.* Many writers encounter problems with this basic rule because they rarely read documents with strong evidentiary support. If you are accustomed to reading the opinion page in newspapers, to reading political blogs on the Internet, or to watching personality-driven news television shows, then you are not accustomed to arguments supported by evidence. Opinion pieces, whether print, web based, or televised, are just that—opinion. The writer or speaker has been hired because he or she has a strong *ethos*—a strong personality. Evidence-based arguments, or *logos,* are not a priority in this type of media. Thus, the primary ways that we encounter arguments these days are poor models for scholarly writing generally and scholarly legal writing in particular.

Just like professional legal writing, scholarly legal writing places a strong emphasis on evidence and authority. If you glance at a page from a law journal, you will notice that up to half of the page of text is composed of footnotes. Those footnotes contain evidence supporting the claims that the writer makes in the text. For some readers, the evidence in a law review article is just as important as the claims the writer makes. (If these journal articles have a strange appearance to you, remember that the format and style of law journal articles is highly specialized, governed by Bluebook citation style.)

It is useful to think of evidence as falling into a few different categories: primary versus secondary sources, and scholarly versus nonscholarly sources. Next we will examine each category more closely.

## Primary Versus Secondary Sources

In general, a **primary source** is composed of first-hand testimony, official documents, speeches, letters, diaries, and any item that makes up "the thing" you are studying. If you are studying law, then the official legal documents that compose law—that *are* law—are the primary documents.

For example, if you are researching a court opinion, all of the documents pertaining to that opinion are primary: the opinion itself, the transcript of the oral argument, the briefs filed by the parties, *amicus* briefs filed by outside groups, the trial transcript, and any other legal document related to the case. These are your objects of study—"the things" you are studying. (Chapter 6 describes these documents in detail tells how to cite them properly in MLA and APA styles.)

If a primary source is the actual thing you are studying, then a **secondary source** is anything written *about* the thing you are studying. If you are studying a court opinion, secondary sources are any journal articles, books, encyclopedia entries, or popular news articles written about the case. The authors of legal secondary sources are usually legal scholars, law students, and journalists. Scholars turn to secondary sources to understand primary sources better. Secondary sources also give a sense of the **scholarly conversation** about a topic: what scholars have already written about it and what the current debates are. You do not want to simply repeat what other scholars have written; learning about the scholarly conversation is a crucial part of your research.

## Scholarly Versus Nonscholarly Sources

Secondary sources can in turn be divided into two types: scholarly sources and nonscholarly sources. This division is not perfect, but here are some guidelines for how to figure out whether a secondary source is scholarly. There are two factors to consider: who the author is and where the piece was published. These two factors work together to determine (1) whether the source is scholarly and (2) how influential, reliable, and strong the source is.

**Scholarly Author?**   For example, say a law professor who specializes in constitutional law published an article on gun control in the *Harvard Law Review*. This source would be a very strong source for our legal writer who is researching the *Heller* opinion. The author is highly influential and reliable as a professor of law who works in the area the writer is focusing on. The publication is also highly influential; it is the number one law journal published by the number one law school in the country.

Sometimes scholars write articles for nonscholarly publications such as newspapers, magazines, and Web sites. Our constitutional law professor might write an editorial for the *New York Times* on gun control and the Constitution. The publication is not scholarly; however, the author is a scholar *writing in his area of expertise*, and the publication is reputable. Thus, our legal writer can use this source to support a claim. It is important to remember, however, that the source published in a popular medium is not nearly as strong as the article published in a law journal. In addition, if this law professor wrote an editorial about his or her vegetable garden, then the source would not be scholarly at all because the author is no longer writing about his or her area of expertise.

**Scholarly Publication?**   Any article published in a scholarly journal is a scholarly source. The strength of the source depends on how well respected the author is. The law professor's article would be more influential than one written by a law student. The law student's piece is still scholarly, however, and may in fact be excellent. Remember: Some law students end up as Supreme Court justices, law professors, and presidents of the United States.

Nonscholarly, or "popular," secondary sources are articles published by nonscholars in nonscholarly magazines. A journalist who writes about a court opinion in the *Washington Post* is not a scholar, and the source is a popular publication, not a scholarly one. You can use nonscholarly sources in your research, but they carry far less weight as evidence for your arguments. Nonscholarly sources are a great way to learn about current events, though, and are also a great place to begin your research before moving on to more scholarly sources.

In sum, the two clues to look for when deciding whether a source is scholarly are (1) the identity of the author and (2) the type of publication. Most of the time, a source only needs to meet *one* of these criteria in order to be considered scholarly.

## COUNTERARGUMENTS AND REBUTTALS

**Counterarguments** are all of the possible arguments that oppose your thesis. You should anticipate them in your writing and provide responses. Responses to counterarguments in which you put to rest the anticipated naysayers of your text are called **rebuttals**. When you provide rebuttals to counterarguments, you are also creating supporting arguments for your thesis. This process of counterargument/rebuttal is best seen in an example, and one of the best examples is a famous speech by former slave and abolitionist Sojourner Truth.

Truth delivered this speech in 1851 at the Women's Convention in Akron, Ohio. In her speech, Truth uses lay language to address complex public policy and legal arguments. She uses counterarguments and rebuttals to frame her supporting arguments. As you read, try to answer these questions:

- What is her thesis?
- What are her three supporting arguments?
- What does she use as evidence?

### "Ain't I a Woman"

*Sojourner Truth*
*Delivered at the Women's Convention in Akron Ohio, 1851*

Well, children, where there is so much racket there must be something out of kilter. I think that 'twixt the negroes of the

South and the women at the North, all talking about rights, the white men will be in a fix pretty soon. But what's all this here talking about?

That man over there says that women need to be helped into carriages, and lifted over ditches, and to have the best place everywhere. Nobody ever helps me into carriages, or over mud-puddles, or gives me any best place! And ain't I a woman? Look at me! Look at my arm! I have ploughed and planted, and gathered into barns, and no man could head me! And ain't I a woman? I could work as much and eat as much as a man—when I could get it—and bear the lash as well! And ain't I a woman? I have borne thirteen children, and seen most all sold off to slavery, and when I cried out with my mother's grief, none but Jesus heard me! And ain't I a woman?

Then they talk about this thing in the head; what's this they call it? [member of audience whispers, "intellect"] That's it, honey. What's that got to do with women's rights or Negroes' rights? If my cup won't hold but a pint, and yours holds a quart, wouldn't you be mean not to let me have my little half measure full?

Then that little man in black there, he says women can't have as much rights as men, 'cause Christ wasn't a woman! Where did your Christ come from? Where did your Christ come from? From God and a woman! Man had nothing to do with Him. If the first woman God ever made was strong enough to turn the world upside down all alone, these women together ought to be able to turn it back, and get it right side up again! And now they is asking to do it, the men better let them. Obliged to you for hearing me, and now old Sojourner ain't got nothing more to say.

Truth's thesis is not obvious from the text. She does not use one of the signal phrases often employed by scholarly writers. Instead, she makes an observation, one that can be phrased like this: "Given all of the political uproar around the country, something must be wrong." This is the crux of her argument: *Something is wrong*. Many people would have disagreed with her, people who liked the political status quo of 1851 just fine. After making her main claim, she refines it by suggesting that white men will be "in a fix" if they ignore the political uproar, an uproar driven by black people and women seeking civil rights. If we frame her thesis as a scholarly thesis statement, it might look like this: "In this article, I argue that there is serious political turmoil surrounding women's rights and the rights of African Americans, turmoil that white men ignore to their detriment."

What about her supporting arguments and evidence? Truth uses counterarguments to create her supporting arguments. Each of the middle three paragraphs presents a supporting argument framed as a counterargument and rebuttal. The three counterarguments can be stated this way:

(1)  Women are weak.

(2)  Women are unintelligent.

(3)  Women are not reflected in God.

Truth rebuts the first by using evidence of her own body and personal experience—an appeal to *ethos*. Women cannot be weak, she says, because she is strong and has worked hard. She rebuts the second with a classic rhetorical move: the "so what?" strategy. Instead of claiming that women are intelligent, she simply says that intelligence is not relevant to the argument: "What's that got to do with women's rights?" The argument of irrelevancy forces her opponents to justify why their argument matters.

Her last rebuttal refutes the counterargument with syllogistic logic: with an enthymeme. (See Chapter 1 for a review of syllogisms and enthymemes.) Her evidence is the Gospel of the Bible, the story of the birth of Christ.

**Major Premise:** ?
**Minor Premise:** God and a woman created Christ.
**Conclusion:** Women are, indeed, God-like.

The missing major premise goes something like this: "The creator of Christ must necessarily be God-like."

We can reframe her counterarguments and rebuttals as supporting arguments. You can see from this list that Truth made a strong rhetorical choice to use the counterargument framework in this speech:

(1) Women are strong and do not need to be protected from politics (or anything else).

(2) Women are not less intelligent than men, but even if they were, it would be irrelevant to this discussion of civil rights.

(3) Because a woman, Mary, gave birth to Jesus, women are as godly as men.

By framing these arguments as counterarguments, Truth creates a tone that is much more compelling than a direct listing of her arguments.

What is Truth's evidence? For her first argument, she uses personal experience as evidence that women are strong. She lists her physical accomplishments and points out that no man offers her assistance in her daily life. For her second argument, Truth does not provide evidence at all; rather, she dismisses the argument as irrelevant. You might also notice that her second argument seems the weakest of the three, and this could be attributed to a lack of evidence. For her third argument, she uses the Bible as evidence, in particular the story of the birth of Christ—and for many in her audience, the Bible was strong evidence, indeed.

In her conclusion, Truth follows the form of a classical peroration, advising the best course of action for her audience based on the arguments she has made in her speech. Her conclusion can be restated in this way: "Our society has problems, and women are strong enough to fix those problems; furthermore, it is in the best interests of men to allow women to do so."

## WRITING AN ARGUMENT OUTLINE

As you can see, Truth's speech is a complex rhetorical creation. Such complicated arguments require advance planning. Each supporting argument, whether framed positively as a supporting argument or negatively as a counterargument, must be supported by evidence. In order to arrange the arguments and evidence of a scholarly paper, it is useful to write an argument outline.

When law students and lawyers write persuasive court documents, they often use a special type of outline to prepare their arguments and research. Sometimes called "point-heading outlines," these outlines contain the various arguments and subarguments the lawyer will address in the document. Each argument or subargument is written as a persuasive sentence. Under each argument and subargument the author provides citations to authority such as case law to support the argument, with relevant language quoted.

The argument outline for scholarly writing serves the same organizational purpose as a point-heading outline by providing persuasively written argument sentences supported by authority. This genre pulls together skills you have learned in this chapter: how to craft a thesis, how to invent arguments using legal *topoi*, and how to support your arguments with appropriate evidence. Once you have a strong argument outline with adequate evidentiary support, you have an organized framework to begin drafting a scholarly paper.

Here are some guidelines for writing an argument outline. (You might need to see Chapter 4, on legal research, and Chapter 6, on citing legal sources, in order to complete this writing project.)

## Step One: Supporting Arguments

Open a blank word processor document. Write your thesis as a full sentence at the top of the page.

Next, under your thesis, start writing a list of possible supporting arguments. Number them. These arguments might be refined as you go on, and you might add some or delete some. The supporting arguments should be written as *complete sentences that make a claim*. Write down any argument that comes to you—do not edit now. You want to have more than you could possibly use in your paper so that you can select the strongest ones.

You might notice that your supporting arguments might have supporting arguments of their own—good! List them as 1-A, 1-B, and so on.

## Step Two: Evidence

Next, under each heading and subheading, you should list possible evidence you will use and explain *how* this evidence supports the argument. First, write out the complete bibliographic entry for each source. (Later, you can just cut and paste these into your references page.)

After you list the source, *describe in detail* what evidence the source provides for your claim. Be as specific as you can. You will probably discover that you need to do more research.

## Step Three: Arrangement and Transitions

Lastly, go through your outline and rearrange supporting arguments so that they flow in a logical order. Be sure to keep the evidence with the arguments as you move them. Then, in between each supporting argument, jot down ideas about a transition, to help you write your transition sentences later.

### Argument Outline Checklist

- Did I provide evidence to support each argument?
- Did I explain in detail how a particular source supports the argument?
- Did I frame each argument as a complete, persuasive sentence?
- Did I provide a correct and complete bibliographic entry for each source I mention?

# 4

# LEGAL RESEARCH FOR NONLAWYERS

As Chapter 3 explains, evidence, or authority, plays an important role in legal writing, both professional and scholarly. This chapter explains how to gather this evidence in an efficient manner. Fortunately, many primary and secondary legal sources are available on the Internet. Some databases are public access, which means that there is no fee for using them. Some are free for students to use, if a university library subscribes to the database. Some law databases—the most popular and the most powerful—are very expensive and are only available to lawyers who pay the subscription fee and to law students who receive free subscriptions. This chapter discusses the first two types of sources: open sources and university subscription sources. They are arranged in order of usefulness. In fact, if you only had access to the first two—LexisNexis Academic and HeinOnline—you could write a strong research paper.

This chapter begins by discussing some general principles of legal research and how to integrate research into your writing process. The chapter then provides a detailed list of databases with instructions for how to use them effectively. At the moment this book is being written, these are some of the best available resources, but online databases evolve over time. If it appears that this book's instructions have become out of date, please ask a research librarian to assist you.

## PRINCIPLES OF LEGAL RESEARCH

What types of documents will you find when you do scholarly legal research? Primary sources include court opinions, transcripts of trials and oral arguments, briefs written by parties and *amici curiae*, ordinances, statutes, constitutions, executive orders, and administrative rules. Secondary sources include articles published in law journals (also called law reviews), articles published in nonlaw scholarly journals, and popular articles about legal topics such as news accounts of trials and other legal events. With so many available forms of research, finding sources that are relevant to your topic can be a challenge. (See Chapter 3 for a discussion of primary and secondary sources.)

## The Citation Trail

Understanding how law works is a key to understanding how legal research databases are organized. The early chapters of this book emphasized a few key concepts of our legal system: the common law, *stare decisis*, and authority. These concepts tell us that history matters to law because prior legal decisions compose law today. They tell us that earlier decisions guide and even control present ones and that prior decisions provide authority for how lawyers argue and judges rule in present cases. In short, the past controls the present, and being able to accurately describe the past makes one's present argument more powerful.

Later cases cite earlier cases, sometimes favorably and sometimes unfavorably. As you will see, some databases keep track of which later cases refer to which earlier cases, how often, and whether these references are positive or negative. The *Lawrence* majority, for example, cited *Roe v. Wade*, *Griswold v. Connecticut*, and *Eisenstadt v. Baird* to support its ruling. They overturned *Bowers v. Hardwick*, making the law created in *Bowers* no long viable.

Citing past authority to make a present argument stronger applies not only to professional legal writing, but also to scholarly legal writing. Law journal articles are cited by newer law journal articles, and the most important law journal articles are cited the most. For this reason, the law journal database HeinOnline, described later, keeps track of when an article is cited by later articles. It also provides hyperlinks to all of these citing works.

You can begin your research with an old case or law journal article and follow the trail of citations to the present. The citation trail is like a family tree for a legal concept: The concept is born in an old case or article, then gives life to later cases and articles, which then give life to even more. You can also begin with a recent article or case and work your way back to the birth of a specific concept. A large part of doing legal research is simply following the citation trail.

## Precision

One of the hallmarks of legal writing is precision. For example, every word of a contract is chosen with the utmost care, and lawyers who draft statutes haggle over even the smallest punctuation mark. Outsiders to law and legal writing often mistake this precision for nit picking, fussiness, or a way to trick clients out of their money. This is a misconception. Legal writers understand the importance of precision, as even the slightest verbal misstep can have terrible consequences for their clients.

### The Price of Precision

A single comma cost Rogers Communications, a Canadian cable television provider, over 1 million dollars in a 2006 contract dispute with a telephone company. Rogers lost because of this sentence:

> This agreement shall be effective from the date it is made and shall continue in force for a period of five (5) years from the date it is made, and thereafter for successive five (5) year terms, unless and until terminated by one year prior notice in writing by either party.

Rogers believed that the first five years of the deal were secured, but the telephone company argued that they could cancel at any time—even within the first five years—with one year's notice. The court agreed with the telephone company.

The problem centered on the second comma—the one between "terms" and "unless." The second comma rendered the phrase "and thereafter for successive five (5) year terms" a mere interruption of this sentence:

> The agreement shall be effective from the date it is made and shall continue in force for a period of five (5) years from the date it is made unless and until terminated by one year prior notice in writing by either party.

Without the comma, Rogers would have won because the cancellation clause would have only kicked in *after* the first five years had elapsed. It would have applied only to the "successful five (5) year terms," not to the first five years.

In legal writing, precision of quotation and citation are as important as precision in all other parts of the writing process. This yearning for precision is evident in the complexity of *The Bluebook*, which provides hundreds of pages of details for how to cite authority properly.

In order to create precision in citation, most online legal sources have standardized pagination. Standardized pagination allows writers to cite to an exact page number no matter which medium they use—print, PDF, or HMTL. If a database provides the full-text PDF image of a document, the page numbers are the same as they would be in a hard copy. For documents published in HTML format, digital law databases provide page numbers in brackets. Each database has a slightly different format for their bracket numbering, but nearly all provide it. If you would like to see an example of bracket numbering, the excerpt of *Lawrence v. Texas* in Chapter 1 employs it.

When you use legal sources in your writing, double-check all details: the year of the case or statute, the names of the parties, and the page numbers of the material you are quoting. Precision is a convention of legal writing that applies whether you are writing contracts or scholarly articles.

## ONLINE LEGAL RESEARCH TOOLS

What follows is a list of the primary online databases you can use to conduct legal research. These are resources that are available through your library's Web site or to the general public. Not all university libraries have the same databases; yours might have greater or fewer databases than those discussed here.

The best way to use this section is to treat it as a tutorial in online legal research. You should be sitting at a computer with Internet access and with access to your university's library databases if you are a student. Work through the instructions given for each database. Do the suggested practice searches to increase your familiarity with the databases. If you familiarize yourself with these databases now, you will be thankful for your expertise when you have a tight writing deadline.

### LexisNexis Academic

LexisNexis Academic (LNA) is a popular database to which most colleges and universities subscribe. In addition to this common college database, LexisNexis also provides a full-service legal research database to lawyers and other legal professionals with an expensive subscription fee. LNA has a scaled-down version of this professional legal database, but even this scaled-down version has the important sources that most scholars interested in using legal sources might need.

After logging into LNA, you will see a series of tabs at the top of the research window. Select the tab labeled "Legal." (The other tabs, especially the "General" and "News" tabs, are good databases for popular articles on legal topics. These tabs list magazines and newspapers from around the world.) You are now within the Lexis-Legal database of LNA.

The Lexis-Legal database contains most U.S. court opinions and many U.S. law journals. The left-hand sidebar provides the menu for the database. You can search law reviews, federal and state cases, federal and state codes (also called statutes), and the laws of other countries. Let us examine the basic method for searching cases and law journal articles.

**Searching Cases**   In Lexis-Legal, you will have access to many U.S. court opinions, including all of the opinions of the U.S. Supreme Court. To search for a court opinion, go to the left-hand sidebar menu and select "Federal and State Cases." You can search for cases in three ways.

First, you can search by keyword in the big search window. Select the "Natural Language" search, which works a lot like a search in Google or other popular search engines. (If you would like to learn how to use the "terms and connectors" search in Lexis, ask a research librarian to assist you.)

Second, you can search for a specific case using the names of the parties. The "Case Name" search window has two blanks on either side of a "v." Enter the names of the parties in the blank windows. Be aware that there might be more than one case with the same name, so you will need to verify that you have the correct case. The easiest way to verify is to use the date the opinion was decided.

Try it: Type in the words "Lawrence" and "Texas" in the search windows on either side of the "v." How many cases does the search retrieve? Can you find the 2003 opinion that declared sodomy laws to be unconstitutional?

Third, you can search by citation number. The format should be [Volume Number] [Reporter Abbreviation] [Start Page Number]. Chapter 2 gives instruction for how to understand citation numbers. This is the most precise way to pull up a specific case in Lexis-Legal.

Try it: In the citation search window, type in this citation exactly: 539 U.S. 558. Lexis-Legal will take you directly to the beginning of *Lawrence v. Texas.*

**Searching Briefs and Court Documents**    After you have pulled up a court opinion, look to the upper left-hand corner of the screen. There should be a hyperlink that reads "View Available Briefs and Other Documents Related to this Case." Some will be available in Lexis-Legal, but some will not. (Most Supreme Court transcripts and briefs are available through the database Oyez, described later.)

**Searching Law Journals and Reviews**    Lexis-Legal also provides access to all of the top law journals. This is not a full database of *all* law journals, just the big ones. Nevertheless, this database is a good place to start. (For a comprehensive database of *all* law journals, check out HeinOnline, described later.)

To search for law journal articles, select "Law Reviews" from the left-hand sidebar menu. You will see many different options for searching the database, including title of article, author name, and a keyword search. You can also limit your search by date, to ensure that you only pull up the most recent legal scholarship.

**Shepardizing**    One of the greatest research tools in Lexis-Legal is the cross-referencing service called Shepard's Citations. In fact, this research tool is so powerful that lawyers commonly use the word as a verb—to *shepardize*. When you shepardize a case, Lexis will tell you all of the cases that cite or rely upon that case and whether the opinion was overturned or narrowed. The service will also tell you which law review articles have discussed the case, giving you the citations and hyperlinks for the articles.

To shepardize a case, click "Shepard's Citations" in the left-hand sidebar menu. Enter the case citation into the window. At the beginning of the Shepard's page is a summary in a gray box listing the number of cases and law reviews that have cited the case you are searching. You can then scroll down and click links to all of these other sources.

Try it: It might take a while to familiarize yourself with the Shepard's results page, so you should practice now with *Lawrence*. Select the "Shepard's Citations" link in the left-hand sidebar. Enter the citation for *Lawrence*, shepardize the case, and review the results. Can you find the "Prior History"? The "Citing Decisions"? How many law reviews cite the case? Can you figure out what "Positive Analysis" means? What does it mean that *Lawrence* was "distinguished by" other cases? (To learn about *distinguishing*, see the discussion of precedent in Chapter 2.)

# HeinOnline

HeinOnline is another database to which some universities subscribe. If your university has a law school, chances are you have access to HeinOnline. (If your school does not subscribe to HeinOnline, you should use the Law Journal database on LexisNexis Academic. See the American Bar Association Online Law Review Database, discussed later, for a limited public access alternative.)

HeinOnline contains full-text PDFs of most law journals and law reviews published in English around the world. A full-text online document provides an image of the actual printed text of the material. In other words, there is no material difference between a full-text printout of a law journal article from HeinOnline and a photocopy of the hard copy of that article you pulled from a law school's library. (This becomes important when we discuss citation of legal sources in Chapter 6.) After entering the HeinOnline database through your school's account, select "Law Journal Library" from the left-hand column under "Subscribed Libraries." Then select the "Search" tab from the top left-hand corner of the screen. Here, you can search by typing terms in the window. However, this book recommends using the "Advanced Search" search option by clicking the link below the search window. Here you can search by keyword using **Boolean operators** (AND, OR, NOT— they must be in all caps) and limit your search by date to ensure that you are pulling up the most recent scholarly work on your topic.

Once you have entered your search terms, a results page appears. One of the most useful aspects of the search results is the "Cited by" entry. For each article pulled by the search, HeinOnline tells you how many *other* articles cite that source. In this way, the database provides the citation trail for the article. A high number tells you that an article is most likely well respected—or it made many people very angry. You can click the "Cited by" link and see a list of these articles as well.

# American Bar Association Online Law Review Database

Located at **http://www.abanet.org/tech/ltrc/lawreviewsearch.html**, the ABA database provides a search of all of the public access, full-text law journals available on the Internet.

# Google Scholar Advanced Search

Google has recently added a legal search engine to its Google Scholar Advanced Search page. To use this search engine, go to the basic Google Scholar search page at **http://scholar.google.com**. To the right of the search window is a hyperlink for "Advanced Scholar Search." Click this link.

Scroll down to the bottom of the page, and you will find a heading called "Legal opinions and journals." Here, you can limit your search to certain states' laws, to federal laws, and to law journals.

Google now provides the full text—with page numbers—of many court opinions and plans to provide them all. Google is thus an excellent, open-access resource for legal scholars.

# Oyez and Justia

Oyez (pronounced "oy-yay") is a public access Web site located at **http://www.oyez.org**. Oyez only catalogs U.S. Supreme Court opinions. If you are searching for an opinion decided by a different court, use LexisNexis Academic or FindLaw (described later).

Oyez has a Web page of information on every Supreme Court case in history. The site tells you which judges decided the case and provides a brief of the case. There are links to the text of each opinion. Often, Oyez will provide a transcript of the oral arguments and even an audio file (usually an MP3) if one is available so that you can actually listen to the lawyers and judges argue the case. For example, on the case page for *Lawrence*, you will find a short case brief and links to supporting documents, including audio files of the oral argument and opinion announcement. In the "Case Basics" box located on the bottom left-hand corner of the page, the citation number of the case is a link that takes you to Justia.

Justia (**http://www.justia.com**) is a public access database. Their mission statement is "To make legal information and resources free and easy to find." As you can imagine, this is a great resource for beginning legal writers. On the Justia home page, you can scroll down to the bottom half of the page and find a section called "Legal Research & Law Practice." Here, you can search cases, codes, law journals, and blogs. The Justia site also hosts all of the U.S. Supreme Court opinions online in their "Supreme Court Center" (**http://supreme.justia.com**). Justia provides not only the text of the opinion, but also a list of online resources.

On the right-hand side of the screen, you will find links to PDF downloads of the case, to blogs that discuss the case, and to news articles that discuss the case. If you want to learn about a Supreme Court opinion, the Justia page is a great place to start.

## Findlaw.com

FindLaw (**http://www.findlaw.com**) is a free access Web site owned by a large legal publisher, Thomson Reuters. It provides networking for lawyers and clients. For our purposes, it provides a limited free library of cases and statutes on its "legal professional" site (**http://lp.findlaw.com**). After navigating to the professional site, you will find a "Research the Law" search window on the main page. The database contains opinions from the federal courts and from some state courts. You can also click the "Cases and Codes" button in the menu at the top of the home page for more search options. Here you can find a variety of state resources and codes, regulations, and statutes. FindLaw does not have everything in its database, but it has a lot and is free to use.

## Library of Congress Law Library

The Library of Congress (LOC) Law library is a public access collection of resources available at **http://www.loc.gov/law**. The LOC hosts a wealth of historical legal documents, constitutions, treaties, and international primary legal sources. There are also current legal news sites linked here, which make it a great place to start looking for research topics. To get started, go to the left-hand sidebar menu and click "Find Legal Resources." The Find Legal Resources home page has a detailed list of the materials you can find, including a wealth of international resources and a database of legal blogs ("blawgs") which sorts the blogs by topic area.

The LOC also provides the THOMAS database (**http://thomas.loc. gov**) in order to "make federal legislative information freely available to the public." This database specifically indexes the work of Congress.

## Cornell University Legal Information Institute

The Cornell University Legal Information Institute (LII) is available at **http://www.law.cornell.edu**. It is a public access database, providing public legal information. The LII has published all U.S. Supreme Court opinions since 1992 and another 600 significant cases from the whole history of the court (and they are expanding their holdings regularly). They publish the complete U.S. Code—the federal statutes—in an easy-to-read format. In addition, they also offer a variety of secondary sources that would be helpful in discovering topics for research. Their "Law About" menu provides an introduction to many different areas of law, which is great for those new to legal research and writing.

## Wikipedia

Wikipedia is a wonderful resource, and most Internet users are familiar with it. It is best used as a starting place for locating resources that will assist in your research process. For the purposes of academic research, however, Wikipedia fails the "reliable source" test. The main reason why Wikipedia is not a reliable source for scholarly research is that there is no way to determine the credibility of the author, since anyone, anywhere can modify an entry.

Despite this drawback, Wikipedia does have a variety of important uses for legal research. The Wikipedia page for a case gives a quick rundown on the common knowledge available on important subjects and persons relating to court cases. Major Supreme Court cases often have strong entries, which provide the citation number, the full names of the parties, and background details. If you want to verify the citation of a case, just type the case name into Wikipedia. At the bottom of an entry page, there are hyperlinks to other sources. Many of these other sources *are* scholarly; in this way Wikipedia functions as a free database of sources on your topic. There are also links to supporting documents such as trial and oral argument transcripts and briefs filed by the parties, if these documents are available in public databases.

In sum, Wikipedia is a great place to start your research, but details from the site should never be relied upon in legal writing without verification.

## Federal Courts

Federal courts often have their own Web site at **http://www.uscourts. gov**. Start here if you need to learn more about the federal court system. The U.S. court system also provides an online database, called PACER, but they charge money for it, stating, "The United States Congress has given the Judicial Conference of the United States, the judicial governing body of the U.S. Federal Courts, authority to impose user fees for electronic access to case information." (There is currently a debate over PACER fees and whether U.S. citizens should have free access to legal information.)

## State Courts

State court systems in the U.S. have their own Web pages with great resources. For example, the North Carolina courts are located at **http://www.nccourts.gov**. You can then click the link for "Courts" located in the center of the page. Then, on the left-hand side is a link for Supreme Court and appellate court opinions. This brings you to a page with opinions sorted by year, going back more than ten years. Other states have similarly informative Web sites.

## Government Printing Office

The **Government Printing Office** (GPO) is a legislative branch agency that publishes federal statutes (including the *Statutes at Large*; see Chapter 6) and most documents of the legislative, judicial, and executive branches. Its public Web site, the Federal Digital System (called *FDsys*, located at **http://www.gpo.gov/fdsys**), provides wonderful access to all sorts of federal documents from all three branches, including presidential memos, recent federal statutes, and records of congressional hearings. If you are searching for a federal document and are not sure where to find it, start at the GPO.

In addition to the databases listed here, there are many other great resources for legal information on the Internet, including sites hosted by university law libraries and blogs by law professors and practitioners. A simple Internet search for your topic will reveal these other sources. Bookmark them in your browser for future use.

# 5

# WRITING EFFECTIVE PARAGRAPHS

One sign of good legal writing is a strong, well-organized, and well-developed paragraph. In professional legal writing, composing paragraphs (sometimes called "paragraphing") is an important skill. In professional documents such as memos and briefs, the paragraph is the primary means of quickly communicating information to the reader. As a professional legal writing professor explains, "A good piece of legal writing does not require the reader to figure things out for herself" (Dernbach 116). Remember, readers of professional legal documents tend to be busy and impatient, unlikely to comb through a complicated text. Organization is key in making professional documents easy to understand and use, and paragraphs are the building blocks of an organized document. Although the audience of scholarly legal writing tends to be a little less in a hurry, organization is still very important. Scholarly legal writers can learn a lot from the paragraphs used by professional legal writers.

This chapter focuses on writing organized paragraphs. To that end, we will look at some guidelines from the professional legal genres for paragraphing. We will see how these guidelines can help scholarly writers stay organized. Although the guidelines for professional legal writing tend to be strict and uncreative, this book advocates a more flexible approach to paragraphs, one grounded in rhetoric. First, a writer must figure out what information the audience is supposed to learn from a paragraph. Then, the writer must present this information in the most effective way possible, taking into account the needs of the audience.

This book divides paragraphs into categories. These categories are not meant to be proscriptive. Rather, consider them as descriptions of different paragraph *genres*. Each genre of paragraph uses a set of conventions designed to accomplish a certain purpose. This chapter discusses five types of paragraphs:

1. introductory paragraphs,
2. background paragraphs,
3. issue paragraphs,
4. umbrella paragraphs, and
5. conclusion paragraphs.

These minigenres are drawn from frameworks of legal writing and classical rhetoric. (To review these frameworks, see Chapter 3.)

## INTRODUCTORY PARAGRAPH

Your introductory paragraph is special. It is your first chance to make a good impression on your reader, and in addition it is the most-read paragraph of your paper. Introductory paragraphs in scholarly articles help readers decide three things:

1. whether to read more of the article,
2. what sections of the article to focus on, and
3. what sections to skip.

Taking these audience needs into consideration, let us examine the minigenre of the introductory paragraph.

First, let us examine the classical framework to see what it can teach us about writing strong introductions. As we learned in Chapter 3, in classical oratory the introduction of a speech is called an *exordium*. The exordium has two main purposes: It introduces a particular audience to the topic of discussion, and it puts the audience into a receptive frame of mind to hear the speaker's position. The second part of the framework is the *narration*, which provides enough background information for the audience to understand the argument. The third part, the *partition*, divides the argument into manageable parts and provides a "road map" for the speech. To summarize what we learn from the classical framework, the introduction needs to accomplish four tasks:

1. to introduce the audience to the topic and persuade them to listen,
2. to provide some background or context about the topic,
3. to give the speaker's argument, and
4. to divide this argument into smaller parts.

An examination of scholarly writing in a variety of fields across the arts and sciences reveals that scholarly introductions can indeed be classified as a minigenre. There are five components commonly used: title, context, scholarly conversation, thesis, and methodology. Often, these five parts can be presented in one introductory paragraph, especially in papers of ten to twenty pages in length. In longer works, such as law journal articles (often fifty pages or more), the introduction might span many paragraphs and pages. Let us examine each component of this minigenre in more detail and look at some examples.

## Titles

Your project must have a title. Your title has two jobs: (1) enticing a reader to look at your paper and (2) telling your reader exactly what your paper is about. Having a title can also help you remember what the focus of your research should be. Of course, your title should change if the focus of your research changes.

Titles of law journal articles and other articles in the humanities and social sciences have certain characteristics. Many titles have a main title that comes first, with a subtitle after a colon. The title tends to be short and catchy. The subtitle usually gives more specific information about the content of the article. Practice writing titles in this format. Here are some examples, with full works cited as entries in MLA style.

Robertson, John A. "Gestational Burdens and Fetal Status: *Justifying Roe v. Wade.*" *American Journal of Law and Medicine* 13.2 (1987): 189–212. Print.

Fallon, Jr., Richard H. "If Roe Were Overruled: Abortion and the Constitution in a Post-*Roe* World." *St. Louis University Law Journal* 51.2 (2007): 611–653. Print.

Mans, Lori K. "Liability for the Death of a Fetus: Fetal Rights or Women's Rights?" *University of Florida Journal of Law and Public Policy* 15.2 (2004): 295–312. Print.

## Context

The context section comes first in the introduction to a scholarly article. It can be a few sentences in a shorter article and a full paragraph in a longer one. The context section must first capture a reader's attention and then hold that attention by establishing the urgency, relevancy, and originality of your work. Here, you answer the questions "Who Cares?" and "So What?" Let's look at these two tasks—capturing attention and establishing urgency—separately.

**Capture Attention**    It can be useful to think of your first sentence as a "hook" to capture the audience's attention. Your hook should pinpoint the issue and establish urgency. At the same time it must avoid overgeneralization. Overgeneralization is a common problem for beginning writers. Writers want to show that their topics are important, so they write hooks that are too distant from their theses, unprovable, or both.

For example, let's say our writer argues that *District of Columbia v. Heller* (2008), the Supreme Court decision that invalidated the D.C. handgun ban, will invalidate most gun control statutes around the country because of its broad interpretation of the Second Amendment. How might the writer begin the article?

> **Bad Hook:** Gun control has been an important issue for the United States ever since the country was founded.
>
> **Bad Hook** After *Heller*, everyone is worried about gun control laws.
>
> **Good Hook** With the *Heller* decision, the Supreme Court has thrown many other gun control laws into jeopardy.

The first hook is too distant from the writer's topic. This paper is not a history of gun control in the United States. Rather, it is a very focused study of the consequences of a single court decision. The second hook is impossible to prove. We cannot know what "everyone" is thinking. The third hook works because it captures attention and establishes urgency while remaining closely tied to the writer's topic. Furthermore, the use of "many" instead of "all" in referring to the jeopardized gun control laws creates a claim that is easier to prove.

**Establish Urgency**    Urgency, or relevancy, can best be understood by examining the ancient rhetorical concept of **kairos** (pronounced kie-rohs). For Greek rhetoricians, *kairos* referred to "time." This was not the kind of time that you read on a clock; their word for that kind of time was *chronos*. Instead, *kairos* referred to a specific point in time, what we might call "timeliness." For rhetoricians, *kairos* referred to the moment when an argument would have the most persuasive power. For example, if the athletic director of a university is interested in raising more money to support the women's basketball team, the best time to ask for this money would be right after the women's team wins the national championship. After the team wins a big game, asking for financial support would be *kairotic* (kie-rot-ic).

*Kairos* is one of the most important considerations for a rhetorician and a scholar. When you write a paper, you make an argument. However, you also have to consider these questions: Why should anyone care about my argument? Is my argument urgent, relevant, and timely? Sometimes the *kairotic* element of your research is obvious. For example, discussing presidential politics in an election year is obviously good timing. Sometimes, however, the *kairos* of your argument is not so easy for your reader to spot.

As a scholar and rhetor, it is your duty to convince your audience that they should read your work. In order to establish that your work is *kairotic*, you must convince readers that your research is timely, urgent, and relevant. In short, you must convince your audience that they should care about your research.

Let us return to our example gun control paper. Here is the hook: "With the *Heller* decision, the Supreme Court has thrown many gun control laws into jeopardy." What should come next? Perhaps the author should mention that the *Heller* decision was issued just last year, demonstrating the timeliness of the article. The writer should mention that new lawsuits are now in the works based on *Heller*, and perhaps name one or two of them, demonstrating that the issue is moving through the courts *right now*. The writer could quote a constitutional law scholar who agrees that *Heller* will have far-reaching consequences. In short, there are many ways to establish *kairos* in an introduction. Keep in mind, however, that a little background information might be necessary, depending on how familiar your audience is with your topic. So a one-sentence summary of *Heller* would be important in this introduction as well.

## Scholarly Conversation

Your opening section establishes the *popular* context of your topic, but in scholarly writing you must also establish *scholarly* context. Scholarly context, sometimes called the **scholarly conversation**, essentially answers this question: "What scholars am I responding to with this research project?" It can be established by discussing names of specific scholars and their claims or by examining specific research trends. Putting a scholarly conversation in your introduction also reassures your readers that you are aware of the research that has already been done on your topic and that you have taken this research into account in your writing. In short, the scholarly conversation tells your readers, "I am an expert on this topic."

In order to discuss the scholarly conversation, you need to do research to discover (1) who are the main scholars in the field that you work with in this piece and (2) what are the main theories that you will be tangling with in your research. Your research does not arise in a vacuum, and you are hardly the first person to write on your topic. In fact, if you are the first person, then you should probably pick a different topic because legal writing depends on following in the footsteps of earlier writers, using what we might call "scholarly precedent."

Many new writers leave out a scholarly context because they are not used to approaching published scholars as an equal. Now is the time to start thinking about yourself as a scholar, too.

In our example on gun control laws, the writer might discuss what constitutional law scholars are saying about the *Heller* opinion and the way it will affect standing gun control laws. The writer might name a scholar by name (constitutional law expert Erwin Chemerinsky suggests that . . .) or name groups or trends (constitutional law experts who agree with the *Heller* holding believe it should be applied broadly, to all gun control laws in the country . . .). There are many ways to show that you are aware of the research that has already been done on your topic and to state your argument in response to this research.

## Thesis

Next comes the thesis section of your introduction. This section has two parts. First, you need to transition from the scholarly conversation (what others are saying) to your thesis statement (what you are saying). This transition sentence or sentences draw a connection between the larger scholarly conversation and your topic. Do you agree with what other scholars are saying? Disagree? Agree with some and disagree with others? Now is the time to let your reader know, *before* delivering your thesis statement.

After this transition comes your thesis statement. As we studied in Chapter 3, thesis statements in law journal articles and other articles in the humanities and social sciences often use signal phrases, such as "This article suggests that," "I suggest that," "This article argues that," or "I argue that."

**Using "I"**   Some of these signal phrases this book provides have the word "I" in them. You might have been taught that you should never use "I" in academic writing. This advice was well meant, but it is wrong. Although some fields frown upon the use of the first person pronoun in academic writing, other fields welcome it, even expect it.

The type of "I" used in the examples just given and that appears often some academic fields is often called a "metadiscursive." **Metadiscourse** is a fancy way of referring to places in a text where a writer talks about the writing, often to direct a reader through the twists and turns of the research. It is those places in a text where the author refers to the text itself, like a tour guide.

In these metadiscursive moments, "I" is a great tool because it lets the reader know that you are stepping outside of your role of researcher and into your role of tour guide. Metadiscursive moments often occur in "umbrella paragraphs," discussed in detail later.

There are less effective uses of "I," and you should avoid these; they are the moments that your high school English teacher warned you about. Some writers use "I" in order to avoid making a strong argument. This is rarely a good idea because using "I" to weaken your position hurts your authority as a writer. A good test for whether you should use "I" or an "I"-phrase is this: Does your sentence work without the "I"-phrase? If you can just delete "I think," "I believe," or "In my opinion" without changing the meaning of the text, then you should.

Remember: Indicating where you stand in relation to other scholars is good. Guiding your readers is good. Using "I" because you are afraid to make a strong statement is not a good idea because it hurts your *ethos*.

## Methodology

The last component of an introductory paragraph is a methodology, which corresponds to the partition section of the classical framework. Your **methodology** is a brief overview of the supporting arguments you will make in your paper, a step-by-step explanation of how you will prove your thesis. You can think of your methodology as a "road map" to your article. You might spend three or four sentences providing this road map.

In the methodology, you will probably use the word "I" again because the methodology is metadiscursive. Here is an example:

> First, I will examine the history of _____. Next, I will examine the implications of _____ for the future of _____. Finally, I will _____.

If your scholarly community allows it, do not be afraid to use "I" when you are explaining the process of your research. Remember, though, to first learn about and follow the conventions for your field regarding the use of "I."

## Assess a Student's Introduction

Now we will examine a sample introductory paragraph written by an undergraduate student named Rachel. Notice how her title is both interesting and explanatory and how she hooks her audience with her first sentence. Can you identify the context in this paper? As you read, try to figure out how Rachel creates *kairos* in her writing. Can you point out key phrases used by Rachel to show that her topic is important? Can you find the thesis section? The methodology?

### Virtual Child Pornography:

When PROTECTing Children Becomes a Constitutional Question

Pedophiles are creating, sharing, and selling images of children engaged in sexual activities, and claiming that this is free speech. The catch is that they are creating these pornographic images using computer software instead of actual children, yet the likenesses are indistinguishable from traditional child pornography. Opponents of regulating virtual child pornography insist that all speech not previously deemed as unprotected by the courts is consequently protected under the First Amendment. I agree, however, with legal scholars who say that there are some new forms of speech, particularly virtual child pornography, which should be included with speech that does not warrant protection. In this paper, I argue that since the Courts have allowed the categorizing of child pornography as unprotected speech, prohibitions against virtual child pornography are also valid under the Constitution. I will first examine the intent of both the First Amendment and previous rulings on child pornography. I will then highlight sections of the Prosecutorial Remedies and Other Tools to End the Exploitation of Children Today (PROTECT) Act of 2003 as it relates to this issue. I will also examine the research of scientists studying pedophilia and the psychological effects of viewing different forms of child pornography. Most importantly I will outline the harms of virtual child pornography in light of our great moral obligation to protect our nation's children. I insist that child pornography, whether virtual or not, is harmful.

Rachel's title is strong. It uses the title/subtitle format well, gives an idea about the topic of the paper, and even makes a play on words, integrating the acronym of an Act of Congress (the PROTECT Act) into the title.

Her hook sentence is also strong: "Pedophiles are creating, sharing, and selling images of children engaged in sexual activities, and claiming that this is free speech." This sentence is both calm and terrifying at the same time because her tone is professional and objective, but the words themselves carry a sense of urgency and even threat. It would be hard not to read on to find out how this threat will be dealt with.

Next she provides some information about the conversation she is entering—who defends virtual child pornography and who does not, and she enters the conversation by writing that she agrees with the opponents. Then she transitions to her thesis statement, and lastly to her methodology.

After such a strong introduction, a reader would choose to read on. However, most readers will need more information about the laws involved in the virtual child pornography debate to understand Rachel's argument. Background paragraphs, discussed next, provide this information.

## BACKGROUND PARAGRAPHS

The second part of the classical framework is the "narration," in which a speaker provides information so that the audience can understand the subject under discussion. In scholarly writing, you will probably need to provide background information for your reader about your topic of research. This information is often conveyed to the audience in background paragraphs.

Background paragraphs do not seem to do a lot of arguing. Instead, they provide necessary background information for your argument. Remember, however, that the way you present background information on your topic can be framed in a way that supports your position.

Why present background information in a separate paragraph? Why not just combine background with arguments? This is a technique that we borrow from professional legal writers. In professional legal writing, the "Facts" section of a document is kept separate from the "Argument" section because it is easier for readers to first read the story of the case and *then* read an analysis of that story. Similarly, in scholarly writing, it is easier for the reader if you first present the information and *then* analyze it.

Background paragraphs in legal writing generally cover one of the following subjects:

1. a case that is central to your project,
2. a piece of legislation, or
3. a historical event.

Generally, a background paragraph is needed when you are going to discuss a highly specialized topic of study, one that you cannot expect your audience to be familiar with. Do not confuse a background paragraph that merely presents information with an analysis paragraph that presents arguments about that information. Keep your background separate from your argument.

A background paragraph often comes right after your introduction, providing enough information so that you can begin your analysis and argument. You might place a second background paragraph, if you have one, later in your paper, when you shift gears to talk about another subtopic of your research.

The topic sentence of a background paragraph often looks like this: "Before we discuss (your argument here), we must review the (name of case/legislation/historical event)." This sentence is a strong **signpost** for your reader, that is, a metadiscursive sentence that guides your reader through your article. Here is an example of a topic sentence for a background paragraph:

> Before we can discuss the negative ramifications of early voting, we must first examine how such programs arose.

This topic sentence is from a background paragraph on the history of early voting legislation in different states. The writer correctly presumes that most of his readers will not be familiar with the legislation that created early voting, so he describes the legislation before defending it in his paper. Here is another example:

> Before we can examine the consequences of school resegregation, we must first examine *Plessy v. Ferguson* (1896) and *Brown v. Board of Education* (1954).

This topic sentence is from a paper about the recent Supreme Court decision *Parents Involved in Community Schools v. Seattle School District No. 1* (2007), which declared public school integration programs on the basis of race—such as busing—unconstitutional. This writer argues that schools will resegregate after the *Seattle* holding, and compares *Seattle* to earlier cases permitting racial segregation by the state. She understands that a background paragraph that summarizes the major holdings of school segregation law will help readers better understand her argument.

A background paragraph generally has a few necessary parts. First, it must have a topic sentence, as discussed previously. Second, you must provide the following:

1. a summary of the people or organizations involved,
2. the date the event occurred or legislation was passed, and
3. a description of the issue or conflict central to the event/legislation/ case.

If you are writing about a case, your background paragraph will look a lot like a case brief put into paragraph form.

It is important to quote the legislation, case, or a historical figure central to the event. It is more fun for your reader to hear a special voice— the voice of a Supreme Court justice, of a U.S. president giving a speech, or of the text of the legislation. Be sure to cite your quotation correctly. (For more on citation of legal sources, see Chapter 6.)

## Assess a Student's Background Paragraph

Once more, let us return to Rachel's paper. This is the background paragraph that follows directly after her introductory paragraph. Notice how she takes time to explain a complicated legal concept, "virtual child pornography." Her topic sentence is strong, and she uses the work of a scholar in the field to teach her readers about this specialized topic of study.

In order to understand why there is so much intense controversy over these questions, we must understand what exactly we are talking about when we refer to "virtual child pornography." Legal scholar Rikki Solowey argues that we should regulate virtual child pornography. Solowey explains that unlike traditional child pornography, computer-generated child pornography does not depict actual living children. Computer-altered images blend pictures of

*(Continued)*

children with pictures of adult bodies engaged in sexual activity. Virtual child pornography is created by morphing an image of an adult's head into that of a child, often using a child's image as the other end of the transition, thereby creating a new image of an unidentifiable child. Solowey points out that the true morphing process actually requires use of a child's image with which to start; therefore, there is an actual living child's image used during the course of production. Computer software also enables the pornographers to shrink the size of genitalia and breasts, remove pubic hair, and slim the bodies of the new images, thus rendering a more youthful, childlike appearance (Solowey 162–163). The computer-generated children are inserted into scenes as engaged participants in sexual activities. This technology is easily accessible and affordable. Even to a trained eye, these computer-generated images are virtually indistinguishable from child pornography that has been produced using living children.

After reading this paragraph, a reader would have a firm grasp of what "virtual child pornography" is and how it is made by pornographers. Notice how Rachel chose a source that describes the facts in an unfavorable light, emphasizing that images of real children are indeed involved in the process, implying that the virtual should be banned along with the real child pornography. In other words, Rachel's presentation of the facts supports her thesis. When you are writing background paragraphs, think of ways to maintain an objective tone while emphasizing facts that support your argument and deemphasizing facts that counter your argument.

## ISSUE PARAGRAPHS

After the introduction and any necessary background paragraphs come the issue paragraphs of your paper. In the issue paragraphs you work through your supporting arguments step by step, following the organization set forth in your methodology. If you wrote an argument outline as described in Chapter 3, a lot of your work is already done—you know what your arguments will be and what sources you will use to support them.

In scholarly legal writing as well as scholarly writing generally, a well-developed issue paragraph has a few common components:

1. a strong topic sentence setting forth the argument of the paragraph,

2. a source or sources that supports the argument of the topic
   sentence,
3. an analysis of this source, and
4. a transition to the next part paragraph.

After you work through all of these steps, you might notice that your paragraphs will grow in length compared to writing you have done in the past. This is good. Do not be afraid of long paragraphs. At the same time, remember the Kraken—the legendary giant sea-beast with eight legs that could pull an entire ship under water. If your paragraph starts growing too long, replete with too many different ideas, it can drown your paper. You might need to remove an idea and start a new paragraph in order to stay organized. In summary, do not be afraid of long paragraphs, but beware the Kraken paragraph.

Here is a summary of four important components often present in strong issue paragraphs. After reviewing these components we will examine a student's issue paragraph to see them in action.

## Topic Sentence

A topic sentence is like a minithesis, presenting the argument of a particular paragraph. Every paragraph needs a topic sentence, which means that every paragraph needs a topic. A topic is a paragraph's reason for being. However, be careful that you only have *one* topic per paragraph. The opening of a paragraph—the topic sentence and perhaps the next sentences as well—needs to accomplish two things:

1. Tell your reader what this paragraph's argument is
2. Situate that argument within the larger context of your paper

## Support from Source

After your topic sentence, and perhaps another sentence or two expanding or explaining the argument of the paragraph, you must support your argument with evidence—usually a primary or scholarly source. This source should be introduced properly and integrated well into your text. (Chapter 6 discusses in detail how to introduce and integrate sources.)

## Summarize/Interpret/Apply

*Summarize/Interpret/Apply (SIA)* refers to the steps a scholar follows in order to make a source support his or her argument. Just plopping a quotation in the middle of your paragraph is not good enough—you must engage with the quotation (or other evidence) and show how it relates to your argument.

First, it helps to *summarize* the quotation for your reader. Yes, your reader did just read the quotation, but your restatement of the author's words using *your* words makes them easier to understand, especially if the source is some highly technical or obscure material. Remember, you had the opportunity to read the words in context, but your reader only sees a snippet. Restating the quotation provides that context.

Next, you need to *interpret* the material for your reader. This means that you need to apply *your* perspective, giving the words the best meaning for your argument. Think about judges and lawyers arguing over the best way to interpret a statute. The statute seems to be written in regular English; why is there so much to dispute? The answer lies in the messiness of language itself. Words and sentences have different meanings for different people because we all bring different perspectives to the text. You need to convince your reader that your interpretation is the best interpretation of the evidence. This requires that you believe in yourself and your ability to understand complicated material.

Lastly, you need to *apply* this interpretation to your larger argument. Here you shift from what the source was saying to what *you* are saying. You might use the word "I" here in order to indicate that you are now putting forward your own argument rather than repeating an argument of a source. You might say that you agree with the source, or disagree, or agree with parts and disagree with other parts.

## Transition

The last sentence of your paragraph should transition to the next paragraph in your paper. Transition sentences and the topic sentences that follow often work together. Sometimes you do not need a transition sentence. The test is whether a reader will be confused by the transition—if the answer is yes, add a transition sentence.

## Assess a Student's Issue Paragraph

Let us return one last time to Rachel's paper and examine an issue paragraph. What do you think of her topic sentence? Does it do all of the things a topic sentence needs to do? Can you point to where she begins the application portion of SIA?

Now that I have shown that the PROTECT Act is constitutional, I will look at the evidence proving why it is also necessary. The risks of protecting virtual child pornography include the negative effects on the viewers themselves, the risk of exposure to children, and the burden to prosecutors. I will first address the negative effects on viewers. Viewing virtual child pornography may create a psychological connection between children and sex where one may not have previously existed. Bryant Paul, professor of telecommunications at Indiana University, and Daniel Linz, professor of psychology at University of California at Santa Barbara, performed experiments with virtual child pornography. Paul and Linz found that "men and women exposed to virtual child pornography or barely legal pornography showed a stronger cognitive association between youth and sexuality than subjects exposed to materials featuring older-looking models" (29). Their research found that the subjects exposed to virtual child pornography were more likely to associate nonsexual images of minors with sexuality. The study shows that societal taboos still enforce inhibitions against sexual relations with youth. However, Paul and Linz posit that continued viewing of child pornography, virtual or otherwise, will likely break down inhibitions, especially if viewers watch enough for emotional desensitization to occur (32). Paul and Linz say that the cognitive consideration of a particular behavior may be the first step toward intentional behavior (34). I assert that harm resulting from desensitization due to viewing virtual child pornography would be magnified by the government condoning of such images. A governmental stamp of acceptability, and thus accessibility without fear of prosecution, upon virtual child pornographic images would lead to increased viewing, which in turn would lead to further desensitization. Thus the protection of virtual child pornography in combination with desensitization would lead to increased cases of pedophilic tendencies.

In this paragraph, Rachel begins by situating this paragraph in the larger argument of her paper using signposts and other metadiscursive tools. She tells the reader exactly what is going on in her argument. She uses the word "I" three times in this opening, but never once does it weaken her argument.

> Now that I have shown that the PROTECT Act is constitutional, I will look at the evidence proving why it is also necessary. The risks of protecting virtual child pornography include the negative effects on the viewers themselves, exposure to children, and the burden to prosecutors. I will first address the negative effects on viewers.

She then presents her evidence—a psychological study that exposed adults to virtual child pornography. After presenting the results of this research, she ties the research to her argument. First, she presents a summary of the evidence *before* she gives the evidence. This is a fine strategy: "Viewing virtual child pornography may create a psychological connection between children and sex where one may not have previously existed."

After giving this summary statement, she goes step by step through the study with strong detail and page numbers for each portion, like this: "Paul and Linz say that the cognitive consideration of a particular behavior may be the first step toward intentional behavior (34)."

Then, she ties the study into her argument: Because of these negative effects, laws should take a strong stance and ban child pornography. She signals to the reader that she is transitioning from the voice of the scholars she quotes to her own voice by using "I": "I assert that harm resulting from desensitization due to viewing virtual child pornography would be magnified by the perceived government condoning of such images."

She ends the paragraph with a strong statement of her position, summarizing and reiterating her argument: "Thus the protection of virtual child pornography in combination with desensitization would lead to increased cases of pedophilic tendencies."

Although there are many tasks that an issue paragraph must accomplish, a writer has great flexibility when it comes to the act of writing. Rachel's paragraph is a strong example, but feel free to experiment in your writing with different ways to tie arguments and evidence together.

## CONCLUSION PARAGRAPHS

In conclusion paragraphs, you summarize your argument, add concluding arguments, and discuss ramifications of your project in a larger scope. Conclusions often move from the *specific*—the topic you discussed in your paper—to the *general*—the larger implications of your findings. As you move from the specific to the general, ask yourself these questions: What are the consequences and implications of the claims I am making? How does the world change because of my work?

Conclusions can be framed in a variety of ways. They often pose questions, exhort some sort of action on the part of the readers, or warn that if a certain action is not followed, negative consequences will ensue.

Some writers find it helpful to return to *kairos* in the conclusion. The question you need to answer in your conclusion is, "Now that I've done this research and persuaded you to agree with my argument, what happens?" This question can be shortened to "Now What?"

Here is Rachel's conclusion paragraph.

I insist that virtually created pornographic images of children are indistinguishable from real child pornography and therefore will yield equivalent harmful outcomes. I dispute the opinion of Judge Donald Molloy in *Free Speech Coalition v. Reno* (1999) when he concluded that, "If there's no real child, then there's no real victim, then there's no real crime" (1096). This type of reasoning identifies the primary criticism of virtual pornography regulation. However, I have shown conclusive evidence that even without the abuse of a child in the original production of virtual child pornography, significant risk does exist for children in the society. The PROTECT Act is narrowly tailored to be an effective solution for the dilemma of virtual child pornography, and it must be upheld against further challenges. There is a lot of debate over the freedom of speech concerning pornography, but it is always centered on the speech of the pornographer. Centering the debate in such a way succeeds in silencing the speech of children, who collectively would raise their voices to say that they do not want to be coerced, sexualized, or victimized in any way due to virtual child pornography. Nevertheless, prohibitions against virtual child pornography will probably be challenged once again. If, in a well-intentioned but misguided effort to guard free speech, the Supreme Court does not heed these arguments and fails to uphold the PROTECT Act, then Congress must be ready to craft and introduce new legislation quickly. Otherwise, we as a nation will have cheapened our children's value by accepting their pornographic sexualization.

Remember, these paragraph genres are not the only paragraphs that exist in scholarly writing. They are simply the most common and the ones that you need to master. In order to learn about the genres of scholarly writing, I suggest you *read scholarly writing*. See if you can spot any other types of paragraphs common in articles in your field.

## ANALYZE AN INTRODUCTION

A student named Kennedy wrote the following introduction. Read it carefully and then work through the questions posed afterward. This exercise will sharpen your ability to recognize the conventions of the minigenre of scholarly introductions and then use those conventions in your own writing.

### "Unequal Laws Unto a Savage Race:"

### The Validity of Student Judicial Evidence in Criminal and Civil Courts

More college students are having criminal charges brought against them than ever before. When a student commits a crime or civil transgression, more often than not he also violates the expectation of good conduct outlined by his university. He is thus subject to two separate forms of discipline: criminal or civil courts and collegiate disciplinary proceedings. This paper will explore the role of student judicial proceedings as they overlap with action taken in criminal or civil courts. Both systems vary radically from each other in terms of procedure, purpose, and rules. However, both systems use similar evidence to exculpate or convict the accused students. In this paper, I argue that evidence discovered in the course of student judicial processes is tainted and otherwise invalid in criminal or civil court until proven otherwise. First, I will analyze what constitutes student records under the Family Educational and Rights and Privacy Act (FERPA, 20 U.S.C. 1232g). I will then examine how and to what extent a prosecuting attorney may obtain such records as evidence, and how it can be used in criminal or civil courts against the student. Lastly, I will analyze the applicable Federal Rules of Evidence in the context of evidence obtained in student judicial processes and the necessary rules for its admission into evidence.

## Questions

(1) How does the writer establish *kairos* in this paragraph? Does the opening sentence hook your attention? Why or why not?

(2) Does the student provide a conversation into which he is entering? Does he discuss what other scholars or writers think about his topic?

(3) What is the student's thesis? Does the writer provide enough introductory material so that you understand what his thesis is arguing?

(4) Does the student's methodology provide a road map for his paper? Does it seem too short? Too long? What if the paper was ten pages long? Forty?

# 6

## USING SOURCES

In the Chapter 1, we developed a definition of legal writing: *the skill of making legal claims and supporting them with authority.* You put this definition into practice in Chapters 1 through 5. You learned how to read and analyze cases, how to find a topic and research the topic using databases, how to organize arguments and authority, and how to put that organization into paragraph form.

Now you will learn how to integrate and cite authority in your writing. You will learn how to cite precisely, keeping in mind the importance of precision in legal writing and research. (For more on precision, see Chapter 4.)

In this chapter we first will examine the rhetorical purposes of citation. We will then examine the basic framework of citation, a framework shared across many citation styles. Next we will learn how to integrate sources into a text. The last part of the chapter provides a list of specialized legal documents that you might want to use in your research, with guidelines for how to cite these documents in Modern Language Association (MLA) and American Psychological Association (APA) styles.

### RHETORICAL PURPOSES OF CITATION

Simply put, a **citation** is a reference to an external source. In legal writing, citing to strong sources, or authority, makes your writing stronger. This principle holds for other fields of research as well. Sometimes the evidence is composed of scientific observations made in a lab, sometimes it is made up of details derived from the close reading of a literary text, and sometimes it is statistical evidence gathered through studies of large groups of people. Every field has its own types of evidence and requires writers to use that evidence to support their claims. If you use evidence in your writing, you must cite it.

There are three main purposes for correctly citing the sources you use in your writing:

- to gain the authority or strength of those sources for yourself, that is, to empower your *ethos* as a writer,
- to give credit to others whose work you are borrowing, and
- to provide a research trail for your readers to follow.

Let us examine each of these purposes separately.

## Gain Authority

If you can point to an established opinion, to the work of an expert in your field, to a strong empirical study, or to a respected source when you make an assertion in your writing, your writing gains the authority of that opinion/study/expert/source. Think of the sources you cite as your teammates—they make your work stronger. However, you have to cite them in order for your reader to know who they are and what they are saying. You already know that in judicial opinions, judges provide lists of references to prior decisions to support their current holding. This is because judge-made law is composed of prior decisions, that is, of precedent. Think of the sources you use in your research as a type of precedent. The cases, law journal articles, and other sources that you use to support your claims are scholarly precedent. You are inheriting a great history of legal thought. Use it in your writing.

One final note: Some new writers worry about the originality of their work. They believe that if they cite other scholars in their research, then their research will not be original enough. Remember, you do not need to create from scratch all of the ideas in your article. In fact, using others' ideas and building upon them makes your writing stronger, like building a house upon a strong foundation.

## Give Credit

Many writers are afraid of **plagiarism**: using another person's original work and claiming it as one's own. Part of the problem with plagiarism is that writers are not always sure what it is exactly. You will never accidentally plagiarize if you remember this principle: *You must give credit for* *ideas that are not yours, no matter whose "words" you use.* Citation is the method for giving credit to the writer whose ideas you are using. There are three different ways that you can use another person's work that requires citation to avoid plagiarism.

**Direct Quotation**    Obviously, if you directly quote someone else's material, you must cite it. In MLA and other styles that use parenthetical citation (more on this later), the parenthetical should come immediately after the quotation, not at the end of the paragraph in which it appears.

**Paraphrase**    A **paraphrase** is a restating of the ideas of another writer or scholar, using a similar number of words as the original. New writers sometimes call this "putting it into my own words," and they mistakenly believe that because the words are different, no citation is required. This is incorrect. A paraphrase *must* be cited. Treat a paraphrase just as you would a quotation, putting the parenthetical with a specific page number immediately after the paraphrase. Remember: Even though you used your own *words*, you still have to cite a paraphrase because you are using someone else's *ideas*.

**Summary of Ideas**    A **summary** is a restatement of a source's ideas; the writer turns a long excerpt of the source text into a much shorter version. Because a summary treats a longer excerpt of original material, it can be hard to cite specific pages. Give a page spread in your parenthetical instead, indicating which pages you used to create your summary.

## Research Trail

The third reason to cite your sources precisely is to leave a research trail for your readers to follow. Readers interested in your work might want to learn more about what you have researched. Accurate citations allow for readers to repeat your research, reading the same primary and secondary sources that you have read, perhaps building on your work. When you are writing a citation, ask yourself, "Can a reader use this citation information and easily repeat my research?" If the answer is "No," then you need to provide more information about your source.

**Hint: "Common Knowledge"**

You might have heard the rule that you do not need to cite "common knowledge." This might sound simple, but the rule is more complicated than it sounds. It is not always easy to determine what knowledge is "common." The problem is rhetorical: The *audience* of a piece of communication determines what is and is not common knowledge. You must be aware of your audience's knowledge about your topic. Usually their knowledge is less than you think it is.

As a general rule, important dates and events that can be found in encyclopedias (such as Wikipedia) are common knowledge. For example, the author and date of the Declaration of Independence are common knowledge. If you quote the exact text of the Declaration, however, you should cite Thomas Jefferson and the book or Web site in which you found the text.

# BASIC CITATION FRAMEWORK

Now that you know *what* to cite, we will learn *how* to cite. Different types of documents use different styles to indicate a citation. You have heard of many of these styles already: MLA, APA, Chicago, and Bluebook. These **citation styles** are systems used by writers to communicate with readers about the sources used in texts.

Professional legal writing uses the *Bluebook* for citing sources. Bluebook style is also used by most law reviews. Bluebook is a highly complex citation style that you will learn during your first year of law school and then spend your legal career mastering. This book does not go into detail about Bluebook format, but you will learn to recognize it when you read cases and law journal articles.

There are literally hundreds of citation styles out there, but the principles and framework of citation hold for most citation styles you will encounter. Whether you are writing about law in a paper in the humanities (philosophy, English) or the social sciences (political science, sociology), you need to know how to cite these specialized documents in a way that meets the demands of your field of research but also makes sense in light of legal communication. Although different fields have their own styles, once you learn the principles of citation, switching from style to style is fairly simple.

As you might already know, MLA citation style, created by the Modern Language Association, is the preferred format for English and composition courses, and many other types of courses too. APA is the preferred format for political science courses. This book suggests that new writers use MLA or APA style to cite their sources.

## Three Parts of Citation

There are three parts to citation that are shared across most citation styles. Each serves a very important function. The three parts are (1) signal, (2) in-text marker, and (3) bibliographic entry.

**Citation Signal**    The **citation signal** is a word or phrase that indicates that the writer is about to quote, paraphrase, or summarize source material. It looks something like this: "In her book _____, the author *suggests* [or *argues* or *writes*] _____."

In MLA and APA, the signal verb is always in the present tense. (See later discussion, under "Integrating Sources," for a list of signal words.) Signal words tell your reader that you are shifting from your thoughts to someone else's thoughts.

**In-Text Marker**    An in-text marker is a bit of text, usually in parentheses or in superscript, inserted after the source material that refers to the bibliographic entry for the source material. A parenthetical in-text marker (used by MLA and APA) usually provides the author's last name and a page number and sometimes the title and/or publication year of the work as well. A superscript in-text marker is usually a footnote or endnote number, which tells the reader to find the citation information either at the bottom of the page or at the end of the text_____.

**Bibliographic Entry**    Many citation styles, including MLA and APA, require you to provide a bibliographic list of works cited at the end of the text. These bibliographic entries are formatted in a very specific way depending on the citation style you are using. The most important thing to remember about the bibliographic entry is that it works in tandem with the in-text marker. The in-text marker tells your reader *how to find* the bibliographic entry_____.

For example, in MLA, the parenthetical might give an author's last name and page number of the quotation. If the reader wants to know more about the work cited, he or she would turn to the bibliography for the text, which lists works alphabetically by author's last name. The bibliographic entry then tells the reader how to find the work in a library or online database. This process—from in-text marker to bibliographic entry to the database where the work can be found—*is* the research trail. If any step breaks down, so does the research trail.

## Legal Sources in Modern Language Association and American Psychological Association Styles

Let us move on to a short introduction to citing legal sources in MLA and APA styles. This list presumes that you are familiar with the basics of MLA and APA, and that you own a citation manual with a full list of MLA or APA rules. A common mistake made by writers new to using legal sources is to copy Bluebook citations directly into their MLA or APA text. Remember, law review articles and court opinions use a different citation style—you must *translate* these citations into MLA or APA format or the format you are using in your writing.

Here are a few guiding principles for citing law journal articles and court opinions, along with some hints and lists of common problems faced by writers new to legal sources. A full list of legal sources comes at the end of the chapter.

**Citing a Law Journal**    Citing a law journal properly requires you to apply the rules of the citation style you are using.

MLA rules require you to put a parenthetical in the text with the author's last name and a page number. The bibliographic entry in the list of works cited has the author's last name and first name, the title of the article in quotation marks, the title of the journal italicized, the volume and issue numbers separated by a period, the year in parentheses, and the page spread.

APA rules require you to put a parenthetical in the text with the author's last name, followed by a comma, the year of the publication, followed by a comma, then p. or pp., followed by the page number or page spread.

---

**Hint: Page Numbers**

As we learned in Chapter 4, giving the precise page number of the material you are quoting is important. If you pull an article

*(Continued)*

from the HeinOnline database, the page numbers are the same as if you were looking at a hard copy of the journal. The articles stored in the LexisNexis database are in HTML, not PDF format. Look for brackets in the text that indicate page breaks of the original document, the number in the brackets in the number of the new page. Make every effort to find the original page numbers of every document you cite.

Suppose we needed to cite an article by Martha C. Nussbaum called "Poets as Judges: Judicial Rhetoric and the Literary Imagination." It was published in the *University of Chicago Law Review* in 1995. The article is located on pages 1477 to 1519 in the fourth issue of the sixty-second volume. Here is how this source might be cited in the text of a research paper using MLA citation style:

Law and literature has become an important field of study, but one with limits. One law professor maintains that "technical legal reasoning, knowledge of law, and the constraints of precedent play a central role in good judging and supply constraints within which the [literary] imagination must work" (Nussbaum 1480).

Note that there is no comma between the name of the author and the page number in the parenthetical. The period comes after the parenthetical, not inside the quotation marks. Be sure to familiarize yourself with the punctuation rules of your citation style. Punctuating correctly falls under the requirement of precision in legal writing. If this parenthetical were written in APA style, it would look like this: (Nussbaum, 1995, p. 1480). Again, note the specific punctuation, and how it differs from MLA.

Let us move on to the bibliographic entry for this article. Following the rules supplied by the MLA, the entry would look like this:

Nussbaum, Martha. "Poets as Judges: Judicial Rhetoric and the Literary Imagination." *University of Chicago Law Review* 62.4 (1995): 1477–1519. Print.

Note the hanging indent and the use of italics when writing the title of the journal. APA entries also employ a hanging indent and italics, but otherwise the entries are very different:

> Nussbaum, M. (1995). Poets as judges: Judicial rhetoric and the literary imagination. *University of Chicago Law Review 62*, 1477–1519.

Here, the author's first name is abbreviated to just the initial. The year of publication follows next in parentheses. The title of the article is given without quotation marks, and the words of the title are not capitalized, except for the first word and the first word of the subtitle, if there is one. Finally, the title of the journal and the volume number are both italicized, and the issue is not given for a journal paginated by volume (rather than by issue).

Let us look more closely at the process of citing law journal articles and examine some common problems new writer's face.

**Common Problems in Citing Law Journals**   Writers new to legal sources encounter a few common problems as they learn to cite these sources. Most of these problems are caused by the transition from Bluebook format to MLA, APA, and other nonlegal citation styles. The first problem arises when a writer gives the first page number rather than the page spread in the bibliographic entry for an article, mimicking Bluebook style. Here is an example in MLA:

> Nussbaum, Martha. "Poets as Judges: Judicial Rhetoric and the Literary Imagination." *University of Chicago Law Review* 62.4 (1995): 1477. Print.

The "1477" here is the first page of the article in the law journal. Although Bluebook only requires only the start page, most common citation styles require the page spread. The second problem occurs when a writer gives the year spread of the volume of a law journal rather than the precise year in which the article was published. This occurs because law journals are published across a school year rather than a calendar year. You must give the precise year that your particular article was published in MLA and APA format. Here is an example in MLA:

Nussbaum, Martha. "Poets as Judges: Judicial Rhetoric and the
   Literary Imagination." *University of Chicago Law Review*
   62.4 (1995–1996): 1477–1519. Print.

In this example, the "1995–1996" should simply be "1995."

A third problem arises when students abbreviate the titles of law reviews using Bluebook rules rather than write the complete title of the law
review as required by MLA and APA. Example:

Nussbaum, Martha. "Poets as Judges: Judicial Rhetoric and the
   Literary Imagination." *U. Chi. L. R.* 62.4 (1995): 1477–1519.
   Print.

Now we will examine the citing of cases, a more complex process
than citing law journal articles.

**Citing a Case in Text**   When you mention a case in the text of
your article, you should treat the case name like the title of a book or
journal, and italicize it. Even if you are using a shortened version of the
case name—e.g. *Plessy* for *Plessy v. Ferguson*—you should italicize the
name. However, if you are writing about Homer Plessy, the person, do
not italicize his name. "*Plessy*" refers to a case. "Plessy" (no italics)
refers to a person.

When you mention a case in your article for the first time, you should
use the abbreviated full name of the case (e.g. *Plessy v. Ferguson*) rather
than the short version (e.g. *Plessy*). Additionally, you should always give
the year of the opinion in parentheses and mention the court that decided
the case. For example:

In *Plessy v. Ferguson* (1896), the Supreme Court held that
racially segregated railway cars did not violate the Equal
Protection Clause.

If you refer to the case in the next sentence, you can simply call it
"*Plessy*." If you need to cite a specific page of a case, because you
quote, paraphrase, or summarize, then you should use an MLA or APA

parenthetical (or whatever type of in-text marker your style requires). Here's an example of a sentence that might follow the one above:

**MLA:** In *Plessy*, the majority writes, "We cannot say that a law which authorizes or even requires the separation of the two races in public conveyances is unreasonable" (550–51).

**APA:** In *Plessy* (1896), the majority writes, "We cannot say that a law which authorizes or even requires the separation of the two races in public conveyances is unreasonable" (550–51).

The parenthetical does not need the case name because the name of the case is given in the sentence. The parenthetical *does* need the exact page numbers of the United States Reports, the book in which the opinion is published. You should *always* get the original page numbers when citing a case, as they are readily and publicly available.

**Bibliographic Entry for a Case** Student handbooks often give a method for citing legal cases that is incorrect. The *MLA Style Manual and Guide to Scholarly Publishing*, published by the Modern Language Association, tells writers to refer to the Bluebook when writing an article with many legal sources.

APA style resembles Bluebook much more than MLA. The works cited entries for a court opinion look like this:

**MLA:** [Abbreviated Case Name, no underline or italics]. [Volume] [Reporter Abbreviation] [First page number]. [Court name]. [Year Decided]. [Print or Web.]

**APA:** [Abbreviated Case Name, no underline or italics], [Volume] [Reporter Abbreviation] [First page number]. [(Year Decided)].

Here are examples:

**MLA:** Plessy v. Ferguson. 169 U.S. 537. Supreme Court of the United States. 1896. Print.

**APA:** Plessy v. Ferguson, 169 U.S. 537 (1896).

In this works cited entry, the "U.S." refers to the United States Reports, the most reliable book in which Supreme Court opinions are published. If you are citing a Supreme Court opinion, you should always cite to the U.S. Reports, if possible.

**Note:** Although case names are always italicized in the text, in bibliographic entries for both APA and MLA, they are *not* italicized.

**Common Problems in Citing Cases**    There are a few common problems that arise when writers cite cases. First, they often give the docket number rather than the case citation in the bibliographic entry. In fact, student handbooks often suggest providing the docket number. Here is an example in MLA:

> Lawrence v. Texas. Docket No. 02–102. Supreme Court of the
>     United States. 2003. Print.

There are three problems with using the docket number. First, the docket for a case usually refers to many different documents. For example, a single docket number may contain multiple rulings by the court and hence multiple written opinions. Giving the docket number fails the requirement of precision, which is why legal writers do not use it to cite cases. Second, because you are not citing to a specific reporter, you cannot give a page number for material that you quote.

A second common citation problem arises when writers give the name of the judge or justice who authored the opinion as the "author" in the bibliography and parenthetical, like this example in MLA:

> Kennedy, Anthony. Lawrence v. Texas. 539 U.S. 558. Supreme
>     Court of the United States. 2003. Print.

In legal and rhetorical terms, the author of a court opinion is *the court that made the ruling,* not the particular author who wrote the words. New legal writers sometimes believe that they need to specify which part of an opinion they are referring to in the bibliography or parenthetical—the majority, the concurrence, the dissent, or one of multiple dissents if those exist. You can indicate in the text of your article which part of the opinion you are referring to and who authored it, and you should. In your citation of the case, however, you should leave out the name of the authoring judge and whether the opinion is majority, dissent, or concurrence.

## INTEGRATING SOURCES

The use of sources is central to research, but *how* you put those sources in your text is not so simple. In this section, we will learn how to properly introduce and integrate sources into your writing, so that your sources work smoothly with your text and provide the evidentiary support you need. We will examine a student's paragraph step by step as an example.

## Who Is Talking?

The first step in successfully integrating a source into your writing is to discover who the speaker is. Who wrote the article you are citing? Who hosts the Web site? What court authored the opinion, and which judge?

If the source is a law journal article, you should research the identity of the author. Knowing the author's identity can help you determine whether the source is credible and how persuasive the author is. Most law journal articles have a footnote at the very beginning in which the author provides a biographical note. Often, you will see that the author is a law professor or a practicing attorney. You need to verify the biographical information, however, because people change jobs or retire. The simplest way to find a law professor is with an Internet search. Type in the author's name. The first page that often arises is the author's faculty page at the university where he or she teaches. Look for a Web site hosted by a school, one that ends in ".edu." Find out what the author's job title areas of specialty are.

If the article's biographical note states that the author is a "J.D. Candidate," then the author was a law student when the article was published. See if you can discover what the author's current position is. The same rule applies if the author is a judicial clerk, as a clerkship only lasts for one or two years. If the author is a practicing attorney, see if you can find the firm where he or she works and what his or her area of specialty is. If you cannot find biographical information that would add to the author's authority, then refer to the author as "legal scholar."

All of this information helps you establish the strength of the author's authority. In the example we discuss later, we will see how important this authority can be in writing legal scholarship.

## Signal Words

As we learned, when you put a source—a quotation or an idea developed by someone else—in a scholarly paper, there are certain words that you should use to introduce the quotation or idea. For example:

> Thomas Jefferson, in the Declaration of Independence, *asserts* that "all men are created equal."

Signal words indicate to your reader that you are presenting someone else's ideas, shifting from your voice to the voice of a source. They are the key to integrating a source into your writing.

Here are some verbs that you might find helpful.

Table 6.1    Signal Verbs

| | | | |
|---|---|---|---|
| admits | alleges | argues | asserts |
| avows | claims | suggests | contends |
| declares | emphasizes | writes | insists |
| maintains | states | stresses | acknowledges |

### Hint: "Quotes" and "Cites"

Writers often misuse these two verbs when they introduce sources in an article, incorrectly using them as signal words. For example: "Thomas Jefferson, in the Declaration of Independence, *quotes* that 'all men are created equal.'" Or: "Thomas Jefferson, in the Declaration of Independence, *cites* that 'all men are created equal.'" "Quotes" and "cites" do not mean "asserts," "says," "states," or "writes." To *cite* means to reference a source and to *quote* means to use someone else's words.

On a similar note, to *quote* is a verb. If you are referring to someone else's words, you should use the noun *quotation*. (This last rule, however, has nearly been defeated by common usage.)

## Sample Student Paragraph

In an issue paragraph, once you have a topic sentence, an argument, and a source that supports your argument, what do you do? How do you *put that source in your paragraph*? What follows is a sample paragraph from a research paper written by my student Walter. Let us examine how well Walter introduces his source and integrates the evidence into his paragraph.

Here is the full paragraph from Walter's essay, which he wrote using MLA style. The main argument of his research paper is that President Bush and his administration violated rights of Guantanamo detainees guaranteed under the U.S. Constitution. The source that needs to be introduced and integrated is a law journal article that the writer uses to support his own position on the illegality of detaining suspects at Guantanamo Bay, Cuba.

> Before I analyze how the executive branch has denied constitutional rights to detainees at Guantanamo, it is important to establish that the detainees do fall under the protection of the constitution. The Bush Administration has argued in *Rasul* that detainees at Guantanamo fail to fall under the protection of the Constitution due to the lack of sovereignty over Guantanamo. On the contrary, though, I would agree with Gerald Neuman of the *University of Pennsylvania Law Review* who claims that "extraterritorial rights of foreign nationals presumptively arise only in contexts where the United States seeks to impose and enforce its own law" (Neuman 2077). The question then arises of whether the U.S.'s occupation of Guantanamo falls under such terms.

Now, let us analyze each component of this paragraph to see how effectively Walter uses the source in his writing.

**Topic Sentence**    Here is Walter's topic sentence from the paragraph just given: "Before I analyze how the executive branch has denied constitutional rights to detainees at Guantanamo, it is important to establish that the detainees do fall under the protection of the constitution." This topic sentence is strong: It states what the argument of the paragraph will be. Walter uses "I" as a signpost to guide his reader, explaining how this paragraph fits in the larger argument of the paper. (See Chapter 5 for more about using "I" and signposts.)

**Hint: "Constitution" and "constitutional"**

When referring to the U.S. Constitution as a *document*, the word Constitution is always capitalized. On the other hand, the word "constitutional"—an adjective—is not. Nor is "constitution" capitalized when referring in general to constitutional documents. Example: Many countries have constitutions, but not all of these countries can be called democracies.

**Evidentiary Support**    The source that Walter has chosen to use to support this claim, as taken from his Works Cited page, is this:

Neuman, Gerald L. "Extraterritorial Rights and Constitutional Methodology After *Rasul v. Bush.*" *University of Pennsylvania Law Review.* 153.6 (2005): 2073–2083. JSTOR. Web. 5 Mar. 2009.

Here is how the source appears in the paragraph:

The Bush Administration has argued in *Rasul* that detainees at Guantanamo fail to fall under the protection of the Constitution due to the lack of sovereignty over Guantanamo. On the contrary, though, I would agree with Gerald Neuman of the *University of Pennsylvania Law Review* who claims that "extraterritorial rights of foreign nationals presumptively arise only in contexts where the United States seeks to impose and enforce its own law" (Neuman 2077). The question then arises of whether the U.S.'s occupation of Guantanamo falls under such terms.

There are a few problems with this excerpt. The first sentence is good because it sets up the position of the writer's primary opponent in his argument, "the Bush Administration." Also, because Walter referred to the *Rasul* opinion earlier in his paper, it is fine for him to abbreviate the case name in this paragraph. If this were the first mention of the case, then he should write "has argued in *Rasul v. Bush* (2004) that detainees."

The second sentence starts out well, because, after presenting the position of his opponent—the Bush Administration—Walter moves to his position, set up by the signal phrase, "On the contrary." He supports his position with a source, written by Neuman. Instead of introducing his source correctly, however, he writes that Neuman is "of the *University of Pennsylvania Law Review*," which is simply false. Neuman does not work for the *University of Pennsylvania Law Review*, he works for Harvard Law School. There are two points to understand here. First, the title of the journal and the title of the article are *not* usually the best ways to set up a source; instead, you should establish the authority of the speaker of your source by telling *who* the speaker is. Second, in order to know who the speaker is, you must *research* the speaker.

To return to our example: If you do an Internet search of "Gerald Neuman," one of the first links you find is to Gerald Neuman's faculty page at Harvard Law School. Most, if not all, professors have faculty pages hosted by the universities where they teach. The faculty page tells what department a person teaches in, the person's title, and any research or teaching specialties.

In Neuman's case, his title is this: "J. Sinclair Armstrong Professor of International, Foreign, and Comparative Law." This is a long title. Most are shorter. Neuman's probably needs to be shortened before you put it in your paper. This title tells us that he specializes in international law among other things and that he is a prestigious professor because he holds an endowed professorship.

A revision of this excerpt that strongly introduces this source would look like this:

A contrary position is suggested by Gerald Neuman, a professor of international law at Harvard Law School. Neuman claims that "extraterritorial rights of foreign nationals presumptively arise only in contexts where the United States seeks to impose and enforce its own law" (2077).

In this sentence, Neuman is introduced correctly and with enough detail to give him authority on this subject, and the MLA parenthetical is properly formatted, omitting the author's name because it is stated in the sentence.

**Accuracy of Source**   A final point to take into consideration is perhaps the most important of all. You must ensure that you are using a source accurately, that is, that you fully understand what your source is suggesting, and that you are not using material out of context.

The passage in Neuman's article in which this quotation arises is as follows. I have put some key passages in boldface:

> The third alternative, appearing in the *Verdugo* dissents, is what I have called the "mutuality of obligation" approach. **I have defended it** [end 2076, begin 2077] **in my prior work, but I agree that it is not currently the law for foreign nationals.** Roosevelt describes this approach fairly in his article. The mutuality of obligation approach presumes that the extension of U.S. constitutional rights accompanies the assertion of an obligation to obey U.S. law, because the framework of rights is designed to legitimate government's claim to obedience. This correlation between rights and governing authority suggests that constitutional rights should presumptively apply to all persons within U.S. territory, and to all U.S. citizens in any location, **but that extraterritorial rights of foreign nationals presumptively arise only in contexts where the United States seeks to impose and enforce its own law.** It would not necessarily follow that application of a constitutional right produces identical results in domestic and foreign locations—either for citizens or for aliens—given that the operative facts and available alternatives may differ.

Note that Neuman states clearly that the legal option he is about to suggest is *not the law* now. What does this mean for Walter? Neuman's statement cannot be used as an assessment of the current law governing foreign nationals. That means that the sentence "I agree with Neuman's assessment that when the U.S. seeks to apply its own law upon citizens of foreign states, these citizens have rights under U.S. law" must be changed to read "I agree with Neuman's assessment that when the U.S. seeks to apply its own law upon citizens of foreign states, these citizens **should** have rights under U.S. law. However, as Neuman observes, this is not currently the law."

As you might imagine, this factual error disrupts the argument of this paragraph. The entire paragraph must be rewritten. To avoid this problem, you need to *read your source carefully.*

# CITING PRIMARY LEGAL DOCUMENTS

The following citation guidelines supplement the common rules of MLA and APA style.

The guidelines for MLA use MLA rules and draw from Bluebook style when necessary to supplement these rules. Most writing and research handbooks have entries for government documents and documents available online. If there is a legal source you would like to use that is not listed in this book, refer to these entries.

APA, in general, follows the rules for citing legal documents provided in the *Bluebook*. In some ways, this makes APA citation more difficult because you need to be familiar with both APA and Bluebook styles. Here, I provide basic guidelines for APA, but you will need to supplement these guidelines with copies of your own APA style manual and the *Bluebook*.

No matter which citation style you use, keep in mind the three purposes of citation when you are writing your bibliographic entries and parentheticals: to gain authority, to give credit, and to create a research trail.

---

### Hint: Test the Research Trail

If you are not sure whether your bibliographic entry is complete, ask a friend to test the entry for you. Give your friend the bibliographic information and see how easily he or she can find the document online using the information you provide. If your "research trail" is easy to follow, then the citation is most likely correct.

---

The following guidelines are organized around the three branches of government—judicial, legislative, and executive. Thus, court opinions and other court documents come first, legislative materials come next, and executive materials come third.

## Court Opinions and Other Documents

In the United States there are state and federal courts, each with its own rules, and then there are courts of foreign nations with rules of their own. Here are some guidelines for citing the great variety of legal documents out there.

First, let us study the major differences between legal Bluebook citation style and APA and MLA. A common mistake made by scholarly

Table 6.2   Comparison of Citation Styles

|  | MLA | APA | Bluebook |
|---|---|---|---|
| **Book title** | Italicize. Capitalize first letters of major words. | Italicize. Capitalize first letter of first word. | All caps or Small caps. |
| **Book author** | Last name, first name. Plain font. | Last name, first Initial. Plain font. | First name and last name. All caps or small caps |
| **Article title** | In quotation marks. Capitalize first letters of major words. | In quotation marks. Capitalize first letter of first word. | Italicize. Capitalize first letters of major words. |
| **Article author** | Last name, first name. Plain font. | Last name, first initial. Plain font. | First name and last name. Plain font. |
| **Journal title** | Italicize. Capitalize first letters of major words. | Italicize. Capitalize first letters of major words. | All caps or small caps. Often abbreviated. |
| **Case name** | Italics in text, plain in bibliography. | Italics in text, plain in bibliography. | Italics in text, plain in footnote. |

writers new to legal sources is that they mimic Bluebook style rather than following the rules of the citation style of their paper or article. This chart demonstrates some of the most commonly encountered differences between these citation styles. Note how the three styles treat case names similarly. This is because when MLA and APA cite legal sources, they take cues from Bluebook.

In the following sections, this book gives guidelines for citing legal sources in MLA and APA style. This list is not all-inclusive. If you encounter a document that you are uncertain how to cite, remember to follow the rules of your citation style as best as you can and to create a strong research trail.

**Federal Appellate Court Opinions**   As we learned in Chapter 2, when we refer to a "court opinion," we are talking about the written document produced by an appeals court that gives the holding for the case and the reasons for that holding. Both the federal and state judicial systems have appeals courts.

Here is the basic rule for citing a *federal* appellate court opinion, written by a circuit court of appeals or the U.S. Supreme Court:

## Bibliographic Entry

**MLA:** [Abbreviated Case Name, no underline or italics]. [Volume] [Reporter Abbreviation] [First page number]. [Court name]. [Year Decided]. [Print or Web, and database and date if Web.]

**APA:** [Abbreviated Case Name, no underline or italics], [Volume] [Reporter Abbreviation] [First page number]. ([Court Abbreviation if not Supreme Court] [Year Decided]).

## Parenthetical

**MLA:** ([Short Case Name in Italics] [Page#])

**APA:** ([Short Case Name in Italics], [Year Decided], [p. or pp.] [page number(s) cited])

**Note:** In the APA entry for a federal court of appeals, you must provide the circuit number along with the year in the parentheses at the end of the entry, like this: (1st Cir. 1995),or (9th Cir. 2006). This is not necessary for MLA because in MLA you provide the full name of the court as a regular part of an entry for all court opinions.

It is helpful to familiarize yourself with the reporters in which opinions are published. For the Supreme Court, the most reliable (and most cited) reporter is the *United States Reports* (abbreviated *"U.S. Reports"*). You should always cite to the *U.S. Reports*—after all, the Supreme Court does. This is the only official, publicly published reporter. There are two other reporters of Supreme Court opinions, the *Supreme Court Reporter* and the *Lawyer's Edition*, but these are both privately published and less authoritative. Sometimes, however, you need to cite to these secondary reporters. For example, you cannot cite to the *U.S. Reports* if a decision is new. It takes nearly a year for the reporter to publish. You will see citations that have blanks for the page numbers if a case is new. For example, until the 539th volume of the *U.S. Reports* was published, a citation to *Lawrence v. Texas* looked like this: 539 U.S. ____ (2003). If you are using a new case, you should cite to a reporter that has already been published; the *Supreme Court Reporter* is the next-best choice and is published more frequently than the *U.S. Reports*. Page numbers for both reporters, as well as the *Lawyer's Edition*, are provided by LexisNexis.

For federal courts of appeal (also called the circuit courts), opinions are published in the *Federal Reporter*. The *Federal Reporter* is abbreviated as F., F.2d, or F.3d, depending on which "series" you are referring to. The *Federal Reporter*, Third Series (F.3d) has the most recent opinions.

Federal district court opinions (called "orders") are published in the *Federal Supplement* (F. Supp.). For more on the district courts, see "Trial Court Materials," later discussion.

Remember: Do not use the name of the justice who authored the opinion in your works cited page or in the parentheticals. Cite the same way whether you are citing the majority, the dissent, or a concurring opinion—they are all parts of the same case. Simply cite the case, no matter which part of the opinion you are referring to.

**Unpublished Supreme Court Opinions**   U.S. Supreme Court opinions do not appear in the *U.S. Reports* until a year after they have been decided. However, the opinions are available online as **bench opinions** (or **slip opinions**—the terms are synonymous) immediately after they are issued. If you are writing about a very recent case, then you must cite the bench opinion.

The main difference between a bench opinion and an official opinion published in the *U.S. Reports* is this: In the bench opinion, each part of the opinion—majority, dissenting, and concurrence—is numbered separately, starting with Page 1. This means that you must give not only the case name in your parenthetical (if you have not mentioned it in the text), but also the portion of the opinion you are citing.

**Example in MLA**: In *Florida v. Powell* (2010), the U.S. Supreme Court once again considered police *Miranda* warnings, writing that although the "four warnings *Miranda* requires are invariable, . . . this Court has not dictated the words in which the essential information must be conveyed" (Majority Op. 8).

Because the *U.S. Reports* for the case you are citing have not been published yet, you cannot give the starting page number in the bibliographic entry for the opinion. Instead, just type in a blank line. Add a URL to strengthen the research trail.

**Example in MLA**: Florida v. Powell. Bench Opinion. 559 U.S. \_\_\_\_. Supreme Court of the United States. 2010. *Justia.com U.S. Supreme Court Center*. Web. 5 May 2010. Available at: <http://supreme.justia.com/us/559/08-1175/index.html>.

**State Court Appellate Opinions**   State court opinions are usually published in two reporters: a state reporter and a regional reporter. The regional reporters are privately published as part of the National Reporter System and are widely relied upon by lawyers and judges. The state reporters are published by each state and record the appellate opinions of only that state's courts. A citation to either the regional reporter or the state reporter is accurate and authoritative. To cite state appellate opinions, follow the format provided previously for federal appellate court opinions. Here are some examples, in MLA:

**Example citing to state reporter:** State v. Peterson. 337 N.C. 384. Supreme Court of North Carolina. 1994. Print.

**Example citing to regional reporter:** State v. Peterson. 446 S.E.2d 43. Supreme Court of North Carolina. 1994. Print.

The regional reporter here is the *Southeastern Reporter*, Second Series. Note the specific punctuation and spacing used in citing to these reporters to ensure you cite accurately. In APA, you must provide court details along with the year, just like you do for the federal appeals court decisions, but *only when citing to the regional reporter*. In the first example that follows, the reporter name "N.C." tells you that the case is in the Supreme Court because the N.C. reporter only reports Supreme Court opinions. If you are citing to the *Southeastern Reporter*, you must specify the court, as in the second example that follows.

**Citing to state reporter:** State v. Peterson, 337 N.C. 384 (1994).

**Citing to regional reporter:** State v. Peterson. 446 S.E.2d 43 (N.C. 1994).

**Note:** Each state has different rules for how to abbreviate its courts. Please check Bluebook rules when citing to a regional reporter.

**Trial Court Materials** Trial courts produce a variety of documents, but few are widely available in law databases. If you are researching a trial, you might find a trial transcript, a variety of opinions on intermediate matters authored by a judge (often called "orders"), and trial briefs or memos written by lawyers.

For state court materials, cite these documents using the docket number provided by the trial court.

> **MLA:** [Names of Parties]. [Document Name and Date]. [Docket Number]. [Court Name]. [Print or Web, and database (in italics) and date if Web].
>
> **APA:** [Names of Parties], [Document Name and Date], [Docket Number], [Court Name].

Federal district court opinions (called "orders") are published in a reporter called the *Federal Supplement* (*F. Supp.*). For both MLA and APA, citing to the *F. Supp.* reporter is just like citing to the *Federal Reporter*.

In APA, remember to provide the name of the court in the parentheses with the year of the order. For example, (E.D.N.C. 2003), to refer to the Federal District Court for the Eastern District of North Carolina. The *Bluebook* contains a complete list of these abbreviations.

For **trial transcripts**, the precise record of every word spoken at trial, use your parenthetical to cite to the page and line numbers as for "Oral Arguments," as described later.

**Foreign Court Opinions**    Foreign courts use a variety numbering formats to refer to their cases. Citing a foreign opinion requires some creativity on your part. If possible, try to follow the citation formats for U.S. decisions, but use the number system of the foreign courts. This requires a balancing of MLA and APA requirements with the requirements of the foreign court. Fortunately, this balancing tends to be easy to do. Furthermore, in-text parentheticals should be formatted in the same way as for U.S. cases.

Here is the format for a bibliographic entry of a Canadian court opinion:

> **MLA Example:** Caccamo v. The Queen. 1 S.C.R. 786. Supreme Court of Canada. 1975. Judgments of the Supreme Court of Canada. Web. 5 Mar. 2009. Available at: <http://csc.lexum. umontreal.ca/en/1975/1976rcs1-786/1976rcs1-786.html>.
>
> **APA Example:** Caccamo v. The Queen, 1 S.C.R. 786 (1975). Retrieved from: http://csc.lexum.umontreal.ca/en/1975/ 1976rcs1-786/1976rcs1-786.html.

**Petitions and Party Briefs**   When a party wishes to appeal a decision to a higher court, the party first must file a **petition for appeal**. When petitioning the U.S. Supreme Court, this document is called a "petition for **writ of certiorari**." After a court agrees to hear an appeal in a case, the lawyers for the parties write **appellate briefs** (called "briefs") and file them with the court.

These briefs outline the legal arguments for each side and tend to be between twenty-five and fifty pages long. Many briefs are available online and are a way to learn about the legal arguments the parties use to support their positions. Sometimes the court will quote from a brief in its written opinion.

When you cite the petitions and briefs written by the actual parties to the case (not *amicus* briefs—see later discussion for how to cite these), you first give the name of the case, then the name of the brief or petition. The title page of the document will give you the specific title. Give a URL for where the document can be found online to create a strong research trail.

### Bibliographic Entry

**MLA:** Lawrence v. Texas. Petition for Writ of Certiorari. July 16, 2002. 539 U.S. 558. Supreme Court of the United States. 2003. *FindLaw*. Web. 5 Mar. 2009. Available at: <http://supreme.lp.findlaw.com/ supreme_court/briefs/02-102/02-102.pet.pdf>.

**APA Bibliographic Entry:** Lawrence v. Texas. (2002). Petition for Writ of Certiorari. 539 U.S. 558 (2003). Retrieved from: http://supreme.lp.findlaw.com/ supreme_court/briefs/02-102/02-102.pet.pdf.

### Parenthetical

**MLA:** (*Lawrence*, Petition for Writ of Certiorari 22)
**APA:** (*Lawrence*, 2002, Petition for Writ of Certiorari, p. 22)

**Oral Arguments**   Before an appellate court makes a decision in a case, it usually allows the parties to participate in **oral arguments** before the court. This is not a trial; rather, it is a very formal conversation between the attorneys and the judges. The attorneys for the parties take turns, and the arguments usually last about thirty minutes per side. These arguments are transcribed by court reporters. Sometimes an audio recording is made as well. For important cases, these transcripts and audio recordings are made available online. The oral arguments for Supreme Court cases are also recorded, and you can listen to them on Oyez.org. (For more on Oyez.org and other research databases, see Chapter 4.)

The citation format for appellate oral arguments is similar to that for appellate briefs and petitions—the case name comes first. You should give the specific date on which the argument took place and a URL for where a reader can access this information online in order to strengthen your research trail.

For the parenthetical, use the short case name and the phrase "oral argument." Give a page and/or line number if available, and separate by a period.

### Bibliographic Entry

**MLA:** Lawrence v. Texas. Oral Argument. March 26, 2003. 539 U.S. 558. Supreme Court of the United States. 2003. *The Oyez Project*. Web. 5 Mar. 2009. Available at: <http://www.oyez.org/cases/2000-2009/2002/2002_02_102/>.

**APA:** Lawrence v. Texas. (2003). Oral Argument. 539 U.S. 558 (2003). Retrieved from: http://www.oyez.org/cases/2000-2009/2002/2002_02_102/.

### Parenthetical

**MLA:** (Lawrence, Oral Argument 3.14)

**APA:** (Lawrence, 2002, Oral Argument, p. 3.14)

**Amicus Briefs**    Sometimes courts allow outside parties to file briefs with the court in hopes of influencing the court's opinion. These briefs are written by "friends of the court," or *amicus curiae* in Latin. The briefs are simply called "*amicus* **briefs**." Most often, the authors of these briefs are organizations. Sometimes an individual is the author, usually in an official capacity, such as the U.S. secretary of state or the governor of a state. In either case, the name of the actual lawyer who wrote the brief is *not* the name you should give as the author.

Unlike the briefs for the parties, which place the name of the case first, the first thing listed for an *amicus* brief is the organization that sponsored the brief, e.g., NAACP, ACLU, the U.S. Navy, or some other legal activism group. (However, do not use acronyms in your bibliographic entry.) Provide the date, which is often located on the last page of the transcript. Give a URL if the brief is available online to strengthen your research trail.

In the parenthetical, put the author's name along with the page number. If you set up an abbreviation or acronym in your text, then you *can* abbreviate it in your parenthetical. To set up the abbreviation in the text, you simply put the abbreviation in parentheses after your first mention of the organization, like this: "In their *amicus* brief for the *Hamdan* case, the American Civil Liberties Union (ACLU) argues that. . . ."

## Bibliographic Entry

**MLA:** American Civil Liberties Union. Brief Amicus Curiae of the American Civil Liberties Union in Support of Petitioner. January 4, 2006. Hamdan v. Rumsfeld. 548 U.S. 557. Supreme Court of the United States. 2006. *ACLU.org*. Web. 5 Mar. 2009. Available at: <http://www.aclu.org/scotus/2005/hamdanv.rumsfeld05184/23395lgl20060104.html>.

**APA:** American Civil Liberties Union. (2006). Brief amicus curiae of the American Civil Liberties Union in support of petitioner. Hamdan v. Rumsfeld. 548 U.S. 557 (2006). Retrieved from: http://www.aclu.org/scotus/2005/hamdanv.rumsfeld05184/23395lgl20060104.html.

## Parenthetical

**MLA:** (ACLU 22)

**APA:** (ACLU, 2006, p. 22)

# Legislative Materials

**U.S. Constitution**    For both MLA and APA, you should cite the specific part of the U.S. Constitution that you use in your paper. If you use multiple parts of the Constitution, then you will have multiple entries in your works cited page. Cite the article, the section, and the clause if there is one.

**APA:** Constitution of the United States. Full Faith and Credit Clause. Art. IV, Sec. 1. Retrieved from: http://en.wikisource.org/wiki/Constitution_of_the_united_states

**MLA:** Constitution of the United States. Full Faith and Credit Clause. Art. IV, Sec. 1. *Wikisource*. Web. 5 Mar. 2009. Available at: <http://en.wikisource.org/wiki/Constitution_of_the_united_states>

**Parenthetical for APA and MLA:** (Constitution of U.S., Art. IV, Sec. 1)

**State or Foreign Constitutions**   If you are discussing the constitution of another country or of one the U.S. states, try to follow the rules for the U.S. Constitution as closely as possible. Give the article and section number in the parentheticals. Provide a Web site if you found the document online to strengthen your research trail.

**Bibliographic Entry:** [State (or Country) Name]. [Document Name]. [Date Ratified].

**Example in APA:** California, State of. Constitution of the State of California. Art. I, Sec. 3. 1849. Retrieved from: http://www.sos.ca.gov/archives/level3_const1849txt.html.

**Parenthetical:** ([State or country name], Constitution [article and section].

**Example:** (California, Constitution Art. I, Sec. 3)

MLA format for the bibliographic entry is the same, except that you must add the information for your online retrieval of the document.

**Federal Statutes**   **Federal statutes** are laws passed by both houses of Congress—the House of Representatives and the Senate. After Congress passes a statute, the president must then sign it into law. Citing federal statutes is difficult because they are published three times: first, as "slip laws" published individually as they are passed; second, in the *Statutes at Large* volumes published annually; third, in the *United States Code*, published every six years.

Here is how the publication process works. After the president signs the legislation, the Government Printing Office (GPO) publishes the laws as pamphlets called "slip laws." At the end of each year, the GPO publishes all of that year's slip law statutes in the *Statutes at Large* (SAL). The SAL publishes the laws in chronological order. At this point the laws are called "session laws."

The Office of the Law Revision Counsel, an agency of the House of Representatives, "codifies" the new laws in the SAL every six years, integrating them into the *United States Code* (USC). The USC is divided into 50 "titles," or sections, organized by topic. Because a single act of Congress might cover many different topics, the act is divided into parts when it is codified, and each part is filed under its proper topic in the *Code*.

The USC is the preferred citation source for federal statutes. You should provide the title number (1 through 50), then "U.S.C.", then "Sec." followed by the section number. If the law has not been codified, then cite to the SAL, which is abbreviated "Stat." in citations. If you cite to the SAL, you must also provide the Public Law number of the statute. Fortunately, for famous acts of Congress, Wikipedia provides the SAL and Public Law numbers as well as the full titles of the acts. (For more on how to use *Wikipedia* wisely, see Chapter 4.)

According to the *Bluebook*, you may also cite codified laws to the SAL if the act is "scattered" throughout the USC because the act covers a broad range of topics. For both USC and SAL citations, you must also give the full name of the act (if there is one) and the date of enactment. Add a URL to strengthen the research trail.

**Format for USC:** [Statute Name, and title if necessary]. [Title number] U.S.C. [Section number]. [Year enacted].

**Example in APA:** Civil Rights Act of 1964, Title VII. 42 U.S.C. Sec. 2000e. July 2, 1964. Retrieved from: http://www.law.cornell.edu/uscode/.

**Format for SAL:** [Statute Name, and title if necessary]. Pub. L. [Number here]. [Date of enactment]. [Volume number] Stat. [Statutes at Large number]. [Year enacted].

**Example in APA:** Civil Rights Act of 1964. Pub. L. 88-352. 78 Stat. 241. July 2, 1964.

MLA format is the same, except that you must add the information for your online retrieval of the document.

In your parenthetical you can abbreviate the name of the act if you set up the abbreviation in the text. You can set up an abbreviation the first time you mention the name of the act. Right after the full name, in parentheses, put the abbreviation. In the parenthetical, be sure to give the subsection number of the section you quote.

> "The Civil Rights Act of 1964 (CRA) established that. . . ." (CRA Sec.2000e-1)

The GPO Web site provides access to the *Statutes at Large* online, but only for the years that have yet to be codified. You can access the *United States Code* through Cornell University's Legal Information Institute database. Information on both of these web sites is provided in Chapter 4.

**State Statutes and Local Ordinances**   Cite state statutes to the codification of that state's laws. Follow the format as for federal statutes. Local **ordinances** are laws passed by city and county governments. A fine way to cite ordinances is to treat them as online or government documents using MLA or APA style. See your style handbook for guidelines for citing online or government documents.

## International Law and Treaties

International organizations such as the United Nations and the International Monetary Fund often publish documents and agreements that are legally significant. **Treaties** are international agreements between two or more nations. Make your best effort to find the text of the **treaty** online and cite to that to create a strong research trail. If possible, cite to the text of the treaty published on a Web site hosted by the treaty's sponsoring organization.

For international agreements and treaties, you should give the sponsoring organization name (if there is one) as the author's name, the title of the agreement, and the date it was passed. You also should give a URL where the document can be accessed to strengthen your research trail. If possible, use a URL hosted by the organization that actually wrote the document because that Web site will be most authoritative.

In the parenthetical, give the organization name as the author, and give the exact Web location of the document that you are citing.

**Example of International Organization Document in MLA:** United Nations. *Kyoto Protocol to the United Nations Framework Convention on Climate Change.* 1998. United Nations. Web. 5 Mar. 2009. Available at: <http://unfccc.int/resource/docs/convkp/kpeng.html>.

**Parenthetical:** (United Nations Art. I, Sec. 5)

**Example of Treaty in APA:** Comprehensive Nuclear Test Ban Treaty. 1996. Comprehensive Nuclear Test Ban Treaty Organization. Retrieved from: http://www.ctbto.org/the-treaty/.

**Parenthetical:** (CNTBT, 1996, Art. II, Sec. 1)

## Foreign Laws

When you cite foreign laws, you should cite them as closely as possible to the way the foreign country cites them. Give the country name as the author, the name of the law if there is one (and translate into English), the number of the law if the country numbers them, and the date it was enacted. Provide a URL for the law, in translation if possible, to strengthen the research trail.

Use the country name as the author in the parenthetical. Be sure to include article and section numbers if they exist.

**Example in APA:** France. Loi No. 2004–228 du 15 mars 2004 encadrant, en application du principe de laïcité, le port de signes ou de tenues manifestant une appartenance religieuse dans les écoles, collèges et lycées publics. Law No. 2004–228, enacted March 15, 2004, concerning, as an application of the principle of secularity, the wearing of religious symbols or garb in public schools. Retrieved from: http://www.legifrance.gouv.fr/affichTexte.do?cidTexte=JORFTEXT000000417977&dateTexte=.

**Example:** (France, Art. I, Sec. 2)

## Executive Materials

**Executive Orders**    An **Executive Order** is an order issued by the president of the United States. An order has the force of law if its contents lie within the discretion, or power, of the president. Give the name of the president who issued the order as the author, the order number, and the date it was signed. Provide a URL for where the order can be found online to strengthen your research trail. A government-hosted URL is most authoritative and reliable. You can recognize a government-hosted a Web site because it ends in ".gov."

**Example in APA:** Kennedy, John F. Executive Order 10925. March 6, 1961. Retrieved from: http://www.eeoc.gov/abouteeoc/ 35th/thelaw/eo-10925.html>.
**Parenthetical:** (Kennedy, 1961, Sec. 301).

**Administrative Regulations**    **Administrative regulations** are rules issued by government agencies. Most federal agencies fall under the executive branch. Of these agencies, there are two main types. The first are often called "independent" agencies. The president appoints the heads of these agencies. They include the Federal Communications Commission, the Securities and Exchange Commission, and the Fair Trade Commission. The second type includes the executive departments. The heads of these departments are part of the president's cabinet, including the Departments of the Treasury, Defense, and Agriculture. Regulations passed by agencies are published in the *Code of Federal Regulations* (CFR in citation), and this is the book you should cite to. You should cite the most recent edition of the CFR in your bibliographic entry. In your parenthetical, you can use the accepted abbreviation of the agency name so long as you set up that abbreviation in your text. As you can see from the following example, the parenthetical should contain the specific citation to the CFR.

**Example in APA:** Federal Communications Commission. Broadcast Radio Services. 47 C.F.R. Sec. 73.201 (1999).

**Parenthetical:** "The Federal Communications Commission (FCC) regulates all radio broadcasts in the U.S. These regulations stipulate that the FM broadcast bad be divided into one hundred channels (FCC, 47 C.F.R. Sec. 73.201)."

# TRY IT: RESEARCHING AND CITING LEGAL SOURCES

Practice your citation skills by writing the bibliographic entries for the following documents. You will need to find the source first, most likely online, using the legal research skills you learned in Chapter 4. Then, write a correct citation in either APA or MLA using the guidelines in this chapter.

## Example

1. The Due Process Clause

Constitution of the United States. Due Process Clause. Amd. XIV, Sec. 1.

## Now You Try It

**Hint:** First figure out what *type* of document this is, and then refer to that section of this chapter for citation guidelines.

(1) The Establishment Clause

(2) The Sarbanes-Oxley Act

(3) The Geneva Protocol of 1925

(4) *Roe v. Wade* opinion by the Supreme Court

(5) Any *amicus* brief authored for the U.S. Supreme Court case *District of Columbia v. Heller* (2008)

(6) The oral argument of the U.S. Supreme Court case *McCleskey v. Kemp* (1987)

# 7

# PEER WORKSHOPS
# AND REVISION

At this point in your research and writing process, you have read and briefed cases, researched primary and secondary legal sources, written an argument outline, and drafted your paper. Although this seems like a lot of work, you are far from finished. Now you must revise and edit your writing. For many writers, this is the hardest part of their writing process. This chapter aims to ease the difficult task of revision by listing some common errors to look for in your writing and describing general revision principles to help you make your writing stronger.

This book has three main recommendations for successful revision. First, start on your writing early so that you have time to revise before your deadline. Second, let some time elapse between your first draft and your revision so that you can look at your writing with fresh eyes. Third, get others to help you with your revision by having them read and comment on your writing. These recommendations will reappear throughout this chapter because they are crucial to successful revision.

Just as writing is fundamentally a rhetorical task, so is revision. Many of the suggestions in this chapter are framed in terms of audience, for example: "What should the audience learn from a passage of your writing?" "Will the audience grasp your argument, given the complexity of legal discourse?" Remember, if a member of your audience, reading in good faith, misunderstands your writing, *you* must take the blame. Be grateful when a reader admits to misunderstanding your writing because then you have the opportunity to repair the confusing text.

Given the importance of audience in the revision process, working with readers during revision can be crucial. For this reason, many writing teachers require students to work in groups, or "workshops," to read and revise each other's writing. Many professional writers work with readers as well, trading manuscripts before they are published as articles or books. There is nothing more valuable to a writer than a good reader. For this reason, a large part of this chapter is devoted to working with readers during revision.

The chapter first presents quirks of legal discourse that often trip up writers who are new to writing about law. The second section provides tips that will improve scholarly writing in any academic field. The third section coaches you through the process of revising your writing. The last section provides guidelines for working with a writing group and conducting a peer workshop.

## QUIRKS OF LEGAL DISCOURSE

There are many problems common to writers new to scholarly writing, especially writers who engage with unfamiliar topics such as law. Legal topics seem particularly prone to mishandling by writers. In their efforts to tackle advanced legal concepts in their writing, some writers accidentally turn their language into jargon-filled, imprecise, convoluted garble. This often happens because students try to mimic the legal language that fills and often confuses court opinions, briefs, contracts, statutes, and other legal documents. These writers mistakenly believe that if their writing sounds complicated, then they will impress their audience by sounding more "legal."

**Legalese** is a general term that refers to the legal jargon and syntax that clogs and confuses legal documents. It is composed of a variety of language quirks. For example, lawyers like to use paired synonyms and prepositional phrases when single words will do. They also prefer the specific jargon of their field when there are common words that mean the same thing. In addition, they prefer to use nominalizations or passive verbs instead of active verbs.

There is absolutely no need to try to complicate or "legalize" your language in order to sound like a legal expert. The best legal writers use language that nonlegal experts can easily understand. In fact, in the last 40 years, legal writing has undergone a renaissance called the **Plain English movement**. In the 1970s, the federal government began encouraging rule writers to use less bureaucratic and foggy language. More recently, on June 1, 1998, President Clinton released a "Memorandum on Plain Language in Government Writing" in which he expressed the need to "make the Government more responsive, accessible, and understandable in its communications with the public" (1010). Accordingly, Clinton directs, "The Federal Government's writing must be in plain language" (1010). The authors of many, if not most, of these government documents are lawyers.

The Plain English movement is sweeping through the legal profession as well. Plain English signifies a rhetorical shift in legal writing, a shift from the writer to the reader. No longer are lawyers supposed to write for an audience of lawyers, people just like themselves. Instead, legal writers recognize that their audiences are much larger, encompassing many who have not attended law school.

In order to bring Plain English into your scholarly writing about law, keep in mind your target audience, which consists of scholarly colleagues and academics who might read your writing in a scholarly journal. Thus, your audience is not just a professor who assigned a paper. Furthermore, you are not writing a paper just for yourself or someone like you, a reader with expertise in your subject matter. Many members of your scholarly community will be unfamiliar with advanced legal concepts and vocabulary. How can you be sure that you have used Plain English to explain a complex legal concept? Ask yourself, "How would I explain this concept to a scholarly colleague in a conversation?" Try the "roommate test." Have your roommate, spouse, friend, or colleague read the passage you are concerned about. Then, have them explain to you, in their own words, what they think the passage means. How accurate is their explanation? Here are some common problems that arise in writing about law. The first few problems are common to legalese, and you should strive to eradicate them from your writing. The others are common misunderstandings and misusages committed by writers new to legal discourse.

## Paired Synonyms

One of the most baffling aspects of legal writing is the use of doublets, also called paired synonyms. **Paired synonyms** occur when a writer puts two words together that mean the same thing, joined by "and," like this:

cease and desist
free and clear
give and bequeath
heirs and assigns
last will and testament
revoke and cancel
to have and to hold

Lawyers' tendency to use paired synonyms is one of the most often-mocked aspects of legal language.

There are a few theories for why lawyers write in this way. The first theory blames doublets on the Norman invasion of England. Lawyers were forced to pair a French word with an English word so that all parties to a legal action could understand what was happening. This theory does not explain all common paired synonyms, however, as some pairs are derived from two English words or two French words. The second explanation claims that the pairings sound formal, important, and even poetic, and lawyers favor them for how they sound.

The third explanation suggests that lawyers use paired synonyms because they are loathe to change; they keep copying the language of their forebears, and their forebears used paired synonyms. Lawyers believe that what has worked in the past will work in the present.

## Prepositional Phrases

Lawyers often use prepositional phrases when a single word will do. For example:

> Our client is unwilling to consider the offer at the present moment, but may be interested at a later time.

This example has more than one needless prepositional phrase. Here it is, rewritten with the phrases replaced by single words:

> Our client will not consider the offer now, but may be interested later.

Here is a list of phrases and their replacements:

> at the present moment = now
> at a later time = later
> is unwilling to = will not

The first and second phrases are prepositional phrases. Replacing needless prepositional phrases with single words will make your writing elegant and easier for your audience to understand. The third phrase employs a nominalized verb, another common style problem of legal writing, which we will examine next.

## Nominalized and Passive Verbs

**Nominalized verbs** occur when a writer transforms a verb into a noun, then uses some form of the verb "to be" to create a sentence. For example:

> The bicyclist was in a collision with a car.

The verb of this sentence is "was," a form of the verb "to be." A strong revision of this sentence would turn the nominalization back into a verb:

> The bicyclist collided with a car.

This sentence has the added advantage of using fewer words and being easier to follow. Most readers would also agree that the action of second sentence creates an image in the reader's mind—a visual imprint—helping the reader remember the contents of the passage.

A **passive verbs** is the past participle of a verb combined with some form of "to be." Sentences with passive verbs can be confusing because the subject of the sentence is either missing or placed at the end of the sentence in a prepositional phrase. In this example, the subject is missing:

> Joe's watch was stolen.

It is unclear from this sentence who stole the watch, and unclearness—or imprecision—in legal writing should be avoided at all costs. In the next example, the subject is placed at the end of the sentence:

> Joe's watch was stolen by Mary.

This sentence should be revised to place Mary in the subject position and to use an active verb, rather than a passive one:

> Mary stole Joe's watch.

Passive verbs are confusing and overly wordy. Avoid them if you can. Sometimes, however, we need to use passive verbs because we do not know who the subject is. If we do not know who stole Joe's watch, then the passive verb construction might work. However, it would be even more precise to write the sentence like this, using an active verb:

> An unknown thief stole Joe's watch.

Writers sometimes use passive verbs because they are striving for politeness. They do not want to name the subject because the tone of the sentence might be accusatory. For example:

> Women are forbidden from joining Augusta National Golf Club.

When you read this sentence, can you tell who has forbidden women to join the golf club? Why might a writer choose to frame a sentence in this way? Perhaps it seems less accusatory, and more polite, than this sentence:

> The male members of Augusta National Golf Club forbid women from joining.

From this sentence a reader knows who the subject is—that is, just who is doing the forbidding. Although the first version might seem less offensive, it is also less precise. As a scholar writing about law, it is your job to make accurate observations. Do not sacrifice accuracy and clarity for the sake of politeness.

If you are a lawyer arguing a point to a judge, however, politeness is arguably as important as precision. Rather than telling a judge, "You ruled incorrectly," a lawyer might say, "The ruling is incorrect." The second version is less accurate because it leaves out the identity of the person who made the ruling (the judge). It is nevertheless preferable to causing offense.

## "Precedent"

Writers new to legal discourse misuse the term *precedent* in a variety of ways. The first has to do with understanding when to use the singular or the plural of the word. In American jurisprudence, "precedent" (singular) refers to all of the cases that influence a current decision of a court. Many different cases (plural) make up a current case's precedent (singular).

In this way, "precedent" is similar to the word "history." Sometimes we say "histories," but more often the word is used in the singular. We don't say "U.S. histories" very often. This issue of a singular that refers to many cases often confuses new legal writers, and they write sentences like this: "To support my thesis, I will study the precedents that led to the *Brown* decision."

Remember: There are many cases that influenced the *Brown* decision, but only one group constituting the precedent. When discussing the prior cases that influence a variety of contemporary cases, "precedents" is fine to use.

The second way that new legal writers misuse "precedent" is by confusing it with other words. Do not confuse "precedent" with "precedence." Although the princes William and Harry of England might be interested in precedence, new legal writers should avoid the word. Furthermore, avoid confusing "precedent" with "president."

## Introducing a Case

When you first mention a case in your writing, you must tell your readers the full name of the case, the year the case was decided, and the name of the court that heard it. Often, new legal writers leave out the year and the name of the court. Remember: It is not obvious from the case name which court heard the case. Be sure to mention whether the Supreme Court, a federal appeals court, or a state court heard the case. For example:

In *Brown v. Board of Education* (1954), the U.S. Supreme Court held that racially segregated schools are inherently unequal.

Putting the year in parentheses gives your reader that piece of information quickly and efficiently. After this initial introduction of a case, using the short case name, *Brown*, is fine.

Note: In APA style, you must give the year in parentheses for *all* sources that you mention, not just court opinions.

## Try It: Writing Plain English

Here is an example of a passage written in legalese. See if you can "translate" it into Plain English:

At the final conclusion of the office meeting, John and Joe were observed departing the building by Mary. John and Joe, after entering a motor vehicle, a 2000 Ford Taurus, were in a collision with another motor vehicle, a small white pickup truck. For the reasons stated herein, John and Joe could not have committed the crime at the bank, which occurred at this same point in time, because they were otherwise engaged in the office meeting and the aftermath of the motor vehicle collision. Mary will attest and swear that the above events occurred and are true.

## TIPS FOR STRONG SCHOLARLY WRITING

This section presents some suggestions for strengthening your scholarly writing. These are not problems specific to legal writing. Rather, these problems are common to the work of new scholarly writers in a variety of fields.

## Topic Sentences and Signposts

Topic sentences and signpost sentences assist your readers as they work through your research paper. These sentences have to do a lot of work: guiding your reader through your paper and connecting the material in a paragraph to your overarching thesis or argument. For new writers, the first sentences of paragraphs are often really the *second* sentences of these paragraphs. In other words, you might need to add a topic sentence in front of the first paragraph sentence you already have.

When you proofread your paper, look at your topic sentences and make sure that they are doing everything they need to be doing. If they are not, add another sentence at the beginning of the paragraph. Later in this chapter, we will discuss reading *only* the topic sentences of your paragraphs to see if they give an adequate summary of your entire paper.

Ask yourself if you need to add a signpost sentence to help your reader see the relationships between your arguments. (See Chapter 5 for more on topic sentences and signposts.)

## "Clearly"

A constitutional law professor once told his students to beware of the word "clear" in a judicial opinion "because the argument that follows will be *anything but.*" This professor meant that legal writers, even Supreme Court justices, rely on the word "clear" to emphasize a point that is actually weak and open for dispute.

"Clearly," "clear" and other words and phrases like them should rarely be used in legal writing. The reason for this is rhetorical. Legal writers make reasoned, thoughtful, and sound arguments about contentious subjects. Rarely is anything in law "clear" or certain.

This rule holds true for scholarly legal writing as well as professional legal writing. If the answers to the questions you examine in your research and writing were "clear," then you would not need to write papers about them. If it were obvious what the holding of a case should be, then the court would never have heard the case in the first place.

Here is the rule about "clearly": *Good legal writers acknowledge subtlety and complexity because the issues they address are complex and contentious, never "clear."*

Here is a list of phrases to avoid:

Clearly / It is clear that

Evidently / It is evident that

Obviously / It is obvious that

Doubtlessly / It is doubtless that / Without a doubt

Apparently / It is apparent that

## Editorial Hyperbole

**Hyperbole** is a tone problem that occurs when a writer exaggerates a position in order to create strong emotional responses in readers. The problem is that the exaggeration is inaccurate, and it can alienate readers who do not agree with the writer's position.

"Editorial hyperbole" is common among writers of editorial pages of newspapers and the hosts of editorial news programs. These speakers implicitly claim to be reporting accurate information—after all, reporting is the job of newspapers and news programs. However, the speakers disrupt the more objective or reasoned tone of news reporting with hyperbole and cause listeners to feel certain emotions, usually outrage or fear, in order to spur them into action.

Editorial hyperbole has no place in scholarly writing, yet new legal writers are often tempted to use it. After all, much scholarly legal writing suggests changes that should be made to our legal system, and evoking strong emotional responses in readers seems an effective way to encourage the adoption of these changes. Furthermore, many of these changes will directly impact the lives of real people, and this impact often creates an emotional reaction.

Remember: As a scholar, you should never sacrifice accuracy for emotion. Strive to keep hyperbole out of your writing.

Here is an example of editorial hyperbole from a student's scholarly paper on drinking age laws:

> Requiring college students to wait until they are twenty-one to drink alcohol is a grave injustice, since they are not allowed to drink at fraternity parties with their friends who are twenty-one.

The hyperbole here lies in the phrase "grave injustice," because this phrase is an exaggeration of the supposed wrongness of the drinking age laws. The use of this hyperbole actually hurts the writer's argument. Rather than sounding like a reasoned paper on drinking age law and policies, it sounds like a letter to the editor of a college newspaper.

The tone you should strive for in your writing is one of **critical distance**, that is, a tone that shows you have enough emotional distance from your material to approach it with a critical and objective eye. Critical distance gives you great authority as an author because your persona is one of objectivity—even if you are not "objective" at all. Editorial hyperbole ruins critical distance by making your arguments sound unreasonable, emotionally driven, and inaccurate.

Returning to the foregoing example, most readers would agree that setting the drinking age at twenty-one is hardly a "grave injustice."

A grave injustice would be executing an innocent person for a murder committed by someone else. The sentence should be rewritten this way:

> Requiring college students to wait until they are twenty-one to drink alcohol creates a social burden, since they are not allowed to drink at fraternity parties with their friends who are twenty-one.

The new phrase "creates a social burden," although less emotionally driven, gives the author more credibility because it is more accurate and more easily proven.

## Clichés

**Clichés** are phrases that have been overused to the point that they have lost their meaning. For example, what does it mean to "sleep like a baby"? To be "pretty as a picture"? For "blood" to be "thicker than water"? We use these phrases all the time even though their meanings are either inaccurate (babies do not sleep well) or bizarre (discussing the thickness of blood). Because clichés are either inaccurate or vague, you should not use them in scholarly writing.

There are many clichés that address legal topics. Although these clichés originated from some specific factual instance—in our legal system you *are* guilty until proven innocent—writers use them in situations that are inappropriate.

> Justice is blind
> Guilty until proven innocent
> Having your day in court
> The pen is mightier than the sword
> Throwing the first stone

In the following example passage, a writer uses a cliché instead of stating specifically what he means to convey:

> Many social conservatives in the United States condemn doctors who perform abortions, claiming that abortion is murder. However, these conservatives should not throw the first stone because there have been so many murders of abortion doctors by antiabortion activists.

What does this writer mean by "throw the first stone"? It is hard to tell exactly, but probably some sort of argument about how murdering abortion doctors for committing murder is hypocritical. Here, the use of a cliché creates vagueness, and this passage should be rewritten. Here is the revised passage, with the cliché removed. Notice how much more precise the passage becomes:

> Many social conservatives in the United States condemn doctors who perform abortions, claiming that abortion is murder. However, these conservatives are hypocritical when they implicitly endorse the murders of abortion doctors by extreme antiabortion activists.

## Formatting Problems

Many formatting problems can be cured with the appropriate use of your word processor. In this section, this book refers to commands in Microsoft Word. Many of these commands exist in the same or similar form in other word processors, such as Apple Pages and OpenOffice.

**Font**    Choose a font that is compatible across most computer software programs. For example, most computers can display Times New Roman, Arial, Georgia, and Courier New. Using a standard font enables you to share your work with a peer for help with revision. It also enables you to submit your article to a journal editor by email without fear that your font will look poor on the editor's computer.

**Page Break**    Separate your Bibliography or Works Cited page or pages from the rest of your paper by using the "page break" feature of your word processor. A **page break** is an invisible marker in a word processor document that tells a printer to end a page where the page break is inserted, rather than at the end of the actual sheet of paper. If you use a page break, your Works Cited page or pages will always begin at the top of the sheet of paper following the end of your article.

Do not simply use the Enter button to put in spaces until the Works Cited starts on a new page. Although this might look fine on your computer screen, it will often look wrong on other computers because subtle technological changes cause your spacing to change. A page break is a permanent fixture in the text and will open in the same spot no matter whose computer displays your text.

**Headers**   You should put your name and page numbering in the "Header" section of your document. Headers are usually found in the "Insert" menu of a word processor. The text you put in your header will appear on every page of your document.

Remember to check your style manual for the appropriate format for page numbers. MLA requires a header to be flush right (in the top right corner of the page) and contain the author's last name and page number on every page. APA requires your title, written in all caps, be placed flush left and your page numbers be placed flush right.

**Text Alignment**   Do not justify the text of your document. Justification causes the text on the right side of the page to be even vertically, which causes uneven spacing of the words on each line. For example, newspaper columns are justified. You should not justify any documents in legal writing. Many courts and law journals specifically state that text should be flush left only, as do MLA and APA style.

**Hanging Indent**   In MLA and APA styles, a bibliography page must have a hanging indent. A **hanging indent** means that the first line of a paragraph begins at the margin, and then every line after is indented by one half of an inch. Each works-cited entry is its own paragraph.

Some students try to set up the hanging indent using the tab button. If you set up your indent in this way, formatting problems will occur when your text is opened on another computer or if you change your font type or size. Your tab spacing is affected, and your works-cited lines look wrong, with lots of short lines and spaces in the wrong places. Let your word processor indent your text for you.

To set up a hanging indent, highlight all of the entries on your works-cited page. Go to the "Format" menu, then select "Paragraph," and open the large window. Under "Special," select "Hanging Indent." Then set the indent to 0.5?. You can also set up a hanging indent manually, by setting the "first line" indentation to –0.5? and the regular line indent to 0.5".

## REVISION

Many writers dread revision. Instead, you should embrace it. Revision gives you the opportunity to correct any mistakes of thought or language in you writing. It is a second (or third, or fourth) chance to get things right, and rarely in life do we get second chances.

The first step for successful revision is to understand what revision is. Many new writers confuse revision with editing or proofreading. **Revision** is not proofreading; it is an in-depth rethinking of every part of your writing project. "Revision" means to "look again"—to approach the project anew. Only after you have revised do the processes of editing (correcting small spelling, language, and punctuation problems) and proofreading (checking for typos) begin.

The greatest challenge with revision is being able to approach your writing with fresh eyes to make "looking again" possible. In some ways, writers can never look at their writing anew—only outsiders can do that. For this reason, you should ask friends to read your work for you, and accept their comments graciously.

Sometimes you do not have the benefits of revising your writing with a friend, peer, or colleague. If you are revising alone, you have to be your own critic. This is hard to do. Here are three principles to make looking again at your writing easier.

### Start Early

Time is the best advantage you can give yourself in your writing process. Often, writers turn in sloppy work because they have to rush. If you receive a writing assignment, start immediately on research and outline writing. Aim to have a draft written *halfway* through the time allotted for the assignment. In other words, if you are given two weeks to write, spend one week preparing your first draft and the second week revising and editing. This is the "fifty percent" rule of draft writing. On your calendar, mark the assignment due date *and* the fifty percent due date. Then stick to your schedule.

## Create Fresh Eyes

Time can give you fresh eyes on your writing. After you finish your first draft, set the work aside for at least twenty-four hours—the longer the better. When you look at that draft after the passage of time, your errors will become more apparent.

If you do not have time, there are other ways to create freshness. Here are a few suggestions.

**Read Out Loud**    One of the most common pieces of advice given to new writers by teachers and writing center tutors is this: Read your writing *out loud* and *listen* for mistakes. Reading aloud encourages you to read slowly; in addition, you are forced to both listen to and look at your writing. When it comes to revision, two senses work better than one.

**Read Your Topic Sentences**    Go through your paper and read just the first sentence of every paragraph. Better yet, copy your topic sentences onto another sheet of paper so that they form a paragraph. This paragraph should be a good summary of your paper. If it is not, rewrite your topic sentences.

**Use a Ruler**    To make it easier to spot typos and other errors, use a ruler to block out the text below the line you are reading. The ruler keeps you focused on just the words at hand and prevents you from getting distracted by the text to come.

## Use a Revision Checklist

Many writers find it helpful to use a revision checklist. Make your checklist using guidelines you have been given by your professor, your classmates, and assigned readings.

In order to figure out what to look for when revising your writing, start with the assignment sheet given to you by your teacher. The second place to look is in your class notes, where you will have written down (one hopes) any tips and suggestions your teacher has made during the semester. The third place to look is in this textbook and any other writing handbook your teacher has assigned.

Here is a sample revision checklist that you can use or modify to fit your needs. Many writers find it useful to read a draft many times, each time focusing on a different part of the checklist.

**Revision Checklist**

**Introduction**

- Hook
- Scholarly conversation
- Thesis statement
- Methodology

**Paragraph Organization**

- Topic sentence
- Source introduction
- SIA
- Signposts

**Language and Usage**

- Avoid legalese
- Avoid passive and nominalized verbs
- Avoid clichés, hyperbole, and "clearly" words

**MLA Style (or APA, etc.)**

- Parentheticals
- Works-cited entries
- Header: name and page number
- Margins, spacing, fonts

# Get Help from a Friend

The best way to get fresh eyes on your writing is to ask a friend to read all or part of your draft. Recruit your friends, spouse, and roommates—anyone who will agree to your request for a reading.

After you have secured the help of friends, you need to make it easy for them to help you. Print out clean copies of your article, double-spaced so that your friends will have room to write comments. Give plenty of time for a careful reading—a few days, at least. Lastly, you should give your friends a list of specific questions about your text, things they should look for while reading. The writer's checklist just given can be a good place to start when preparing a "reader's checklist" for a friend.

Many colleges and universities have writing centers where tutors are available, often by appointment, to assist students with their writing. You should ask your teacher about your writing center and bookmark the writing center's Web page in your computer browser. Students who use the writing center tend to have fewer typos and better organization. Writing center tutors will not edit or proofread your writing for you; they *will* teach *you* how to do so, which is a far more valuable service.

The next section of this chapter deals with peer workshops, that is, writing groups. Remember: The best way to get friends to read your writing is to offer to read their writing.

## PEER WORKSHOPS

**Writing workshops** are groups of friends or colleagues who get together to read and comment on each other's writing in order to improve their work. Sometimes writing teachers require students to work in peer workshops. If you are asked to work in a group in class to review your writing, or if you choose to meet with a group of students outside of class to work on your papers, here are some guidelines for peer revision that might come in handy.

### Keep Time

Figure out how much total time you want to spend reviewing the work of all group members. Divide this time by the number of writers in your group. Use the stopwatch function on your computer, your watch, or your cell phone. All writers get their allotted time and no more. Group members need to be sure that every writer receives the benefit of the full amount of time by providing lots of observations and suggestions about the writer's text. Sitting in silence is not helpful. Do not be afraid to make suggestions.

### Read Out Loud

To begin, a writer should read the text to be reviewed aloud to the group members. In the ideal case, each writer brings copies of the text for each member of the group. Better yet, you can email each group member your text, and they can follow along on their computers, typing notes as you read. Group members should not interrupt the writer until the writer is finished reading. Instead, group members should take notes on their copies of the text and prepare to give comments. When the writer is finished reading, the group begins the commenting period.

If you are working on a longer paper with your group, you should take turns going through your papers paragraph by paragraph rather than reading an entire paper at once. Work through each group member's paper, one paragraph at a time.

This is a slow process. For example, if each group member receives five minutes per paragraph and there are four people in your group, it will take your group twenty minutes to do one paragraph for each writer. Keep this in mind when planning meeting times for your workshop.

## Give Praise and Criticism

Group members should tell writers both what they did well and what they could do better. Too much of one or the other is unhelpful. Be as specific as you can. While group members are commenting, a writer should keep quiet and not interrupt. Instead, the writer should have a blank piece of paper or a blank document open on a word processor to take notes while the group members make suggestions. Only when the group members are finished can the writer speak again, and then only to ask questions for clarification.

The reason for this rule is simple. Often, when writers receive criticism of their writing, they feel the need to defend their writing and explain why they made mistakes. This is simply a waste of time. There is no need to be defensive when receiving criticism from your group members. Instead, thank them for taking the time to review your work. (If you are unsure what to look for in your group members' writing, review "What To Look For" in the earlier section on self-revision.)

## Specificity

Sometimes it is useful to come to the peer workshop with specific questions for your group members. If you are struggling with your topic sentences, for example, let them know so they can pay special attention to them.

By the same token, when you are commenting on the work of others, the most helpful comments are the ones that offer specific, concrete advice. Telling a writer that a sentence is confusing is helpful. Telling the writer exactly what was confusing about the sentence and how to fix it is far more helpful.

## EDITORIAL ABBREVIATIONS

When reading your paper or someone else's, it is useful to have a shorthand to indicate places that need improvement in the piece of writing. The following is a list of symbols and abbreviations that are commonly used when editing writing. To be most helpful when you use an abbreviation, pair it with a piece of concrete advice for improvement.

Table 7.1   Editorial Abbreviations

| | |
|---|---|
| ¶ | Meaning: Start new paragraph here. Use when a paragraph seems to launch into a new, separate topic or a paragraph seems overly long. |
| arg | Meaning: Argument, argue. For example, you might write, "Good arg." to emphasize the strength of a writer's argument. Tell why you think the argument is strong, too. |
| awk | Meaning: Awkward language. Use if the phrasing just sounds funny or you have trouble understanding the author's meaning. Be specific about the problem, and make suggestions for improvement. |
| clutter | Meaning: Unneeded words that are getting in the way of the point. Clutter is common in writing about law because of the clutter in legalese. Make suggestions for how the writer can trim down language. |
| frag | Meaning: Sentence fragment. Make suggestions for how to create a grammatical sentence. |
| gram | Meaning: Check grammar. Be specific about the grammar problem, and make suggestions for how to fix it. |
| int! | Meaning: Interesting! This is a great way to praise the work of a writer. Tell why the passage is interesting. |
| ital | Meaning: Italicize this text. Most often used when a book, case, or journal title needs to be italicized in the text. |
| unnec | Meaning: Unnecessary. Use when a certain part of the text seems unneeded to get the writer's point across. Be sure to explain why. |
| punct | Meaning: Punctuation problem. Make suggestions for improvement. |
| rep | Meaning: Repetitive. Note when a writer uses the same word too many times close together. It helps to circle the repeated word. |
| sp | Meaning: Spelling problem. Be sure to fix the incorrect spelling. |
| vague | Meaning: Phrase marked is vague or unclear. Sometimes the writer's choice of words or phrases makes for fuzzy writing. Specificity is at the heart of scholarship, especially legal scholarship. Encourage your writing partners to be as specific as they can. |
| w.c. | Meaning: Word choice. Use when the word circled is not the best word or phrase to use. Explain why, and suggest a better word. |

# WORKSHOP CHECKLIST

- Assign a timekeeper.
- Email or trade papers before starting.
- Prepare specific questions for your group members.
- Writer reads; group members take notes.
- Group members comment; writer takes notes.
- Group members provide praise as well as criticism.
- Writer asks follow-up questions if there is time.

# 8

# SHARING YOUR RESEARCH

Because of its practical nature, legal scholarship is meant to be shared with others. Legal scholars not only make observations about the status of law, but they also offer suggestions for how to improve it. In order for these suggestions to have effect, they must be read or heard by an audience, preferably a large one.

There are two primary ways that scholars in a variety of fields share their research: presentations at conferences and publication in scholarly journals. The first part of this chapter focuses on oral presentations. These tips are applicable to class presentations in college or to presentations at scholarly conferences. In other words, these principles of good speaking hold for a variety of oral genres.

The second part of this chapter walks you through the steps of submitting work to a scholarly journal. Undergraduates, graduate students, and professionals out in the "real world" have a variety of venues to which they can submit their research.

## ORAL PRESENTATIONS

Sharing your research with other scholars is an important part of conducting scholarly research. One method of sharing research is to present it at a scholarly conference. A **scholarly conference** is a gathering of scholars—both students and faculty—who share interest in a certain field in order to learn about and present recent research. A conference schedule is composed of long talks by individual speakers, panels with shorter talks by three or four speakers, and roundtables in which a group of speakers share their research with one another, often seated around a table. The first is the most formal, and the third is the least formal. Some conferences have poster presentations in which researchers present their work on a large poster and give short talks to supplement the poster. (The poster presentation is similar to the science fair projects you might have completed in high school.)

If you are interested in presenting at a scholarly conference, you must first find a conference to apply to. If you are a student, your school may have a department to help students who are interested in scholarly research. They can help you find conferences in your area of study. Your professors and advisors can also help you find conferences. An Internet search is yet a third way. Most conferences require you to submit an abstract of your research for approval before you can present. (Later in this chapter you will learn how to write an abstract.)

In contemporary U.S. colleges and universities, the class presentation is the closest students come to a scholarly conference presentation. You must research material, memorize it, and deliver it in an organized and interesting manner.

Whether you are presenting to your class or to a group of scholars, a few common principles of public speaking apply. First, you should keep in mind the rhetorical principles you learned in Chapter 1 of this book, especially the rhetorical triangle. Second, you should maintain strong organization throughout your talk to keep the audience engaged. Third, if you choose to use presentation software, make sure it adds to your talk rather than distracts from it. Given these three principles, let us learn how to give a strong oral presentation.

## Think about Rhetoric

Keep rhetorical strategies in mind when preparing your presentation. The rhetorical triangle helps you figure out who your audience is exactly, what kind of persona (*ethos*) they will best respond to, and what arrangement of material will work best for them. Let us review the rhetorical triangle and see how it can help you prepare a presentation.

**Persona**   A persona is a "face" that a speaker presents to an audience. A persona need not be fake or false; it is simply a way of speaking to which your audience will respond positively. When crafting your persona, think about ways to establish your authority and credibility as a speaker:

- Introduce yourself at the beginning of your talk. Many new speakers forget to do this and just launch into their material.
- To develop your authority, share with your audience anything about yourself that makes you an expert on this material.

- Tell your audience why you chose this topic.
- Dress appropriately for your rhetorical context. Appearance has a huge effect on your authority.

**Audience**    For a class presentation, your audience is actually twofold: your teacher, who is probably grading you, and your classmates, who are hoping to learn something from your presentation. Be sure to keep both audiences in mind when you prepare your material. At a scholarly conference, your audience will be composed of a variety of people. There will be professors and famous experts in your field of study. For new scholars, these experts are often the most intimidating members of the audience. Then there are those who are more like you—young scholars who are new to conferences. There will also be those who are not scholars at all, but rather professionals and other outsiders to the scholarly community. Lastly there will be your friends who have come to support you. Remember, all of these people are there to listen to you speak because they *want* to be there. They are already interested in what you have to say; otherwise they would not have come.

**Purpose**    The purpose of most class presentations is simple: you are supposed to help your classmates better understand the content of your talk. This means that your purpose is not just to impress your teacher. When you sit down to prepare your presentation, ask yourself this question: How can I best help my classmates with my presentation? You can start by making a list of questions you would like to have answered about the material, and then conduct research to answer those questions.

The primary purpose of a conference presentation is to share your research with a wider audience. A secondary purpose is to show others that you are a serious writer and thinker. If you are an undergraduate student, presenting at a conference can help you make contacts in a field you are interested in and improve your chances of getting into graduate school. Graduate students and professionals can impress future employers by participating in a scholarly community. As you can see, there are many good reasons to present at conferences.

## Organization

You might have done great research, practiced your speaking voice, and prepared great note cards, but if your presentation is disorganized, none of these things matter. Here is a simple rule of thumb for presentations: *say everything three times.*

At the beginning of your talk, give a brief **roadmap**, or framework, of what is to come. Then, present the material of your talk. At the end, review in summary form everything you just presented. Throughout your talk, you should use signposts to guide your audience and remind them of the framework of your talk.

An old lawyer's maxim reiterates this process: "When you're talking to a jury, first you say what you're going to say, then you say it, and then you say what you just said."

Here are a few steps to create strong organization.

**Arrange Material**   As you gather your research data for your presentation topic, see if your material will fit into two or three main subtopics. These subtopics will be the foundation of the organization of your presentation. Three subtopics is about all most audiences can keep track of, especially if your talk is thirty minutes or shorter.

**Develop Roadmap**   At the beginning of your presentation, after you introduce yourself and establish your authority, give a roadmap of the main topics you will cover in your presentation. Your roadmap might sound something like this: "First, I will discuss the history of X. Then, I will show how X was received in the media. Lastly, I will explain the influence that X had on Y."

As you can see, this speaker has divided the speech on topic X into these three subtopics: history, media reception, and influence on another issue, Y. (Your speech may have different subtopics, of course.)

**Use Signposts**   During your presentation, you should return to the topics that you presented in your roadmap. When you are finished discussing the first topic, tell your audience that you have finished. Then tell your audience what you are going to cover next. For example: "Now that I have finished discussing the history of X, I will show you how X was received in the media."

**Summarize at the End**   At the end of your presentation, return once more to your roadmap and recap what you discussed.

## Presentation Software Tips

Sometimes you might want to use presentation software, such as Microsoft PowerPoint or OpenOffice Presentation, to supplement your oral presentation. Here are a few guidelines you should keep in mind to make an effective slide show.

**Keep Text Short**    Your slides should supplement your talk, not list everything that you are saying. You do not want your audience to be reading slides instead of listening to you speak. The text should be short phrases, not full sentences. Use bullet points, and limit each slide to a maximum of three bullets.

**Use a Roadmap**    At the beginning of your presentation, after your title slide, you should have a roadmap slide. This slide is basically a table of contents for your presentation. It helps your audience follow you through your presentation and keeps you on track. Try to limit your roadmap to three main topics. As you go through your presentation, use signpost slides to help your audience know where you are in the course of your presentation.

At the end of your presentation, return to your roadmap slide and review everything you discussed in your presentation. Remember the general rule of public speaking: Say everything three times.

**Use Simple Fonts, Colors, and Graphics**    New presentation software is replete with needless frills and decorations. The problem many people face is the tendency to go overboard with fun fonts, graphics, color schemes, and animations. As a rule of thumb, you should use no more than two different fonts and no more than three colors in your entire presentation. Use the same decorative scheme on every slide. Animations and graphics should only be used if they enhance the content of your slide. Remember: Frills can distract your audience from your message.

**Never Read Slides Aloud**    Students and professionals often end up reading their slides to their audiences. It is tempting to use the slides as a script and rely on them too much. Even if they do not read their slides, many people often speak while facing the projector screen and with their backs to their audiences. This is an easy habit to fall into, but you must resist. Speaking with your back to your audience is a delivery *disaster*. You become difficult to hear and understand, and, worst of all, you become boring!

To prevent talking with your back to the audience, print out your presentation and hold the printed version in your hand. Instead of turning around to see where you are, you can simply glance at the paper version. However, do not ignore your slide show. Instead, verify your slide transitions to be sure that you are on the proper slide before you speak; it is okay to make sure your clicker is working properly.

# PUBLISHING YOUR RESEARCH

After you present your research at a scholarly conference, you might be interested in publishing it in a scholarly journal. This section provides guidelines for scholarly publishing.

Publishing your work in a scholarly journal is the ultimate payoff for all of the hard work you have done on your research. Having a scholarly publication on your resume will improve your applications to graduate school, law school, and jobs because admissions people and employers will know that your work is so strong and professional that an outside group chose to publish it. They will also know that you take your work seriously and that you are a hard worker—because publishing is not easy.

There are four steps to scholarly publishing:

- choosing a journal,
- writing an abstract,
- writing a cover letter, and
- sending in your submission.

The more care you give to each of these steps, the higher is the likelihood that your article will be published.

## Research the Journals

The first step in publishing your research is more research. You need to research the journals that might be interested in publishing your work. One of the most common reasons that an article is rejected from a journal is that the journal is not a good fit for the article. In order to be sure that your article is one that a journal would be interested in publishing, start by making a list of journals that (1) publish people like you (e.g., an undergraduate, a graduate student, a professional) and (2) publish research in your field. Some journals say that they publish "student writing," but what that usually means is graduate students, not undergraduates. If you are not sure whether a journal welcomes your writing, email the editor and ask.

Once you have compiled a list of three or four journals that fit your project, find out what their guidelines are. **Writer's guidelines** are the rules that authors must follow when they submit an article to a journal. Guidelines include

- submission deadlines,
- citation style required (MLA, Chicago, APA, Bluebook, etc.),

- word or page length requirements,
- whether your name should be on the article, and
- whether you should submit by email or snail mail.

It is very important that you follow the guidelines given by the journal. If you do not, many editors will just throw your submission away. Most journals have a Web site with guideline information. If you cannot find guidelines, send an email to the editor requesting them.

Once you think you have found a journal that you would like to have publish your research, you need to *read the journal*. Find a hard copy of the journal in your library or see if the journal provides content online. Some journals only exist online, and these are usually free to the public.

Read the table of contents and see if the articles they publish are similar in theme or tone to yours. For example, a history journal might say they are interested in articles about "law," but what they mean is "legal history." If you are writing about a contemporary legal issue, then you should not send your article to that journal.

After you have reviewed the table of contents, read some of these articles. If you start to feel like your work does not belong in this journal, you should find another journal to submit to.

Remember: You can usually only submit to one scholarly journal at a time, so be sure you pick the right one. Once you have selected your journal, you can write your abstract and cover letter.

## Write an Abstract

Your **abstract** is a short document that summarizes the arguments, findings, and conclusions of a scholarly article. The purpose of an abstract is to "sell" your research paper. Scholars use abstracts when they seek to have their research published or to be included in scholarly conferences. Publishers use abstracts to interest readers in their journals; often, an abstract appears at the beginning of an article in a scholarly journal and in online databases.

The length of an abstract can vary. Journal publishers and conference hosts will specify an abstract length in their guidelines. Abstracts usually range from 100 to 500 words. Before you write your abstract, be sure to check to see what length your journal or conference requires.

Generally, an abstract for a legal research paper has five parts. Here is a sample abstract by Rachel, whose paper you are familiar with from the excerpts that appear in Chapter 5. Read the full abstract, and then we will examine it by breaking it down into parts.

**Title:** "Virtual Child Pornography: When PROTECTing Children Becomes a Constitutional Question"

**Author:** Rachel

**Abstract:** Virtual child pornography—pornographic images of children created with computer software instead of live children—has lately arisen as a free speech debate. Because virtual child pornography looks identical to real child pornography, Congress included prohibitions against it in the PROTECT Act of 2003. The constitutionality of the PROTECT Act has already been challenged in the U.S. Supreme Court, and it is likely to be challenged again because of its controversial nature. I argue that because the Courts have allowed the categorizing of real child pornography as unprotected speech, prohibitions against virtual child pornography are also valid under the Constitution. Accordingly, I first I examine several Supreme Court cases, most notably *Osborne v. Ohio* (1990) and *U.S. v. Nolan* (1987), as evidence that child pornography harms all children, even those not involved in the image production. I then present a psychological study of the effects on adults of viewing virtual child pornography. I read this evidence with the ideas of noted feminist Catherine MacKinnon and show that there is ample evidence of the government's compelling interest to classify virtual child pornography as unprotected speech.

Here is the framework of Rachel's abstract, broken down into its components, with suggestions on writing a powerful abstract of your own research.

**Hook**   The first line of your abstract is the most important. Readers use the first line to determine whether they want to keep reading.

Use *kairos* to set up the urgency, relevancy, and uniqueness of your research. This is the first chance you have to get your audience interested in your paper. Here is Rachel's hook:

Virtual child pornography—pornographic images of children created with computer software instead of live children—has lately arisen as a free speech debate.

Rachel has created a strong opening with this sentence. The very first words capture attention, because pornography, child pornography, and "virtual" pornography tend to be inflammatory topics. She also establishes *kairos*, or timeliness, by mentioning that "lately" the Supreme Court has taken up this issue.

**Context**    Your context can be social or scholarly; the best abstracts provide both. Social context describes the public debates surrounding the issue you are writing about. Scholarly context specifically describes what scholars in your field are saying about this topic. The best scholarly writers engage with other scholars in their fields. To provide a scholarly context, you can either name the names of scholars you engage with or explain the scholarly consensus or disagreement on this topic.

Rachel provides social context by describing the legislative and judicial debates surrounding virtual child pornography:

> Because virtual child pornography looks identical to real child pornography, Congress included prohibitions against it in the PROTECT Act of 2003. The constitutionality of the PROTECT Act has already been challenged in the U.S. Supreme Court, and it is likely to be challenged again because of its controversial nature.

She also provides a scholarly context when she specifically names a famous law professor who has written extensively on pornography, Catherine MacKinnon:

> In combining this data with the ideas of noted feminist Catherine MacKinnon, I show that there is ample evidence to support the existence of the government's compelling interest to classify virtual child pornography as unprotected speech.

**Thesis**    In preparing an abstract for a research paper you have already written, you can cut and paste your thesis statement from your paper. See Chapters 3 and 5 for more on developing thesis statements and arguments. Rachel's thesis statement uses a signal phrase, "In this paper," to tell her audience that this is the main argument of her paper:

> In this paper, I argue that because the Courts have allowed the categorizing of real child pornography as unprotected speech, prohibitions against virtual child pornography are also valid under the Constitution.

**Methodology**    You need to include a methodology so that the readers know that you provided strong support for your thesis and that you have organized your work well. Like your thesis, you can cut and paste your methodology from your paper if you wish. Rachel's methodology—-nearly half of her abstract—includes the study of specific cases and the examination of psychological studies on the harm caused by pornography.

> Accordingly, I first I examine several Supreme Court cases, most notably *Osborne v. Ohio* (1990) and *U.S. v. Nolan* (1987), as evidence that child pornography harms all children, even those not involved in the image production. I then present a psychological study of the effects on adults of viewing virtual child pornography. I read this evidence with the ideas of noted feminist Catherine MacKinnon and show that there is ample evidence of the government's compelling interest to classify virtual child pornography as unprotected speech.

**Conclusions**    At the end of your abstract, talk about your findings and their implications. Look at the conclusion paragraph of your paper and see if there is any information there that you can pull into your abstract. Include any recommendations for action that you might have made in your paper. Rachel concludes that "there is ample evidence of the government's compelling interest to classify virtual child pornography as unprotected speech."

After you have prepared your abstract, you are ready to write your cover letter. Your cover letter works in tandem with your abstract to "sell" your article to a journal editor.

## Writing a Cover Letter

On the most basic level, a cover letter simply tells a journal that you are submitting an article for their consideration. In practice, a cover letter convinces the journal editor to consider publishing your article. In an indirect way, your letter tells the editor all of the reasons why the journal should publish your article.

A cover letter is the first piece of your writing that a journal editor will read. If your cover letter is poorly written or unprofessional, then it is highly unlikely that the editor will read your submission.

When writing a cover letter to a journal, the principles of good letter writing apply. Most of us learned how to write a business letter in high school. Use these skills when writing your letter to a journal editor. Your address should be near the top of the page. You can make letterhead in the header of a word processor document with your name, your mailing address, your email address, and your phone number. Provide many ways for the editors to contact you. These days, most editors prefer to use email.

You should address the letter to an individual editor if possible. Often, a journal's Web site will list the names of the editors. Table 8.1 provides some advice for how to address the editor in the salutation.

In the text of your letter, you should italicize the journal's name each time you mention it, just as you would if you mentioned the title of a journal or book in your research paper. Here is a sample cover letter written by a student. Read the letter, and then we will examine each part of the letter separately to identify the key components.

Table 8.1    Cover Letter Salutations

| Editor's Degree or Job | Salutation |
| --- | --- |
| Ph.D., professor | Dear Professor Voltaire |
| Ph.D., but not sure if professor | Dear Dr. Voltaire |
| No Ph.D., but title is "Professor"° | Dear Professor Voltaire |
| No Ph.D. | Dear Mr./Ms. Voltaire |
| Do not know | Dear Mr./Ms. Voltaire |

°Law professors, for example, often do not have Ph.D. degrees.

Kennedy Andrews
PO Box 0000
Chapel Hill, NC 27514
kenn.andrews@uncch.edu
(555) 555-5555

January 1, 2000

Katie Rose Guest Pryal, Editor
*Minerva Undergraduate Law Review*
PO Box 0000
Durham, NC 27701

Dear Prof. Pryal:

Please consider the enclosed manuscript, "'Unequal Laws unto a Savage Race': The Validity of Student Judicial Evidence in Criminal and Civil Courts" (3,445 words), for publication in an upcoming issue of the *Minerva Undergraduate Law Review.* I am a senior at the University of North Carolina at Chapel Hill majoring in history and Italian; my research interests focus on the intersection of student judicial proceedings and civil and criminal trials. This article has never been considered for publication.

The *Minerva Undergraduate Law Review* is the perfect place to publish "'Unequal Laws'" as the article directly addresses the issues of student judicial proceedings and their intersection with criminal and civil law. This work represents the culmination of my four years in a student-run judicial system as both counsel defending students and as a Deputy Student Attorney General charging students with violations under the Honor Code. No other articles address the interaction between evidence collected in student judicial proceedings and the evidentiary rules of civil and criminal courts. This piece provides a close reading of FERPA (Family Educational Rights and Privacy Act), a confusing federal law; furthermore, it applies it to a subject largely untouched by criminal and civil courts.

Attached please find the full article plus a short abstract, in Microsoft Word format. I employed MLA citation style. I welcome any suggestions for revisions that the editorial board may suggest. Please feel free to contact me via email or phone; my contact information is in the letterhead. I thank you for your consideration and await your decision.

Sincerely,

Kennedy Andrews

**Paragraph 1: About You**    The first paragraph of your cover letter needs to tell the editor who you are and that you are submitting an article for consideration. You should also include the following details: what kind of authority you have to write this article, the title of your article, the word count, and whether the article has been previously published elsewhere. Most journals have word limits and do not want to publish work that has been previously published. Some undergraduates worry that they do not have much scholarly authority. It is true that most undergraduates have not completed the schooling or research training that graduate students and professors have. But you should emphasize the authority you do have, as Kennedy does:

> I am a senior at the University of North Carolina at Chapel Hill majoring in history and Italian; my research interests focus on the intersection of student judicial proceedings and civil and criminal trials.

Here, Kennedy talks about where he is in school and his majors, but he also mentions that he has "research interests" and tells what those research interests are. If you have written a major paper on a particular subject, it is fair to say that that subject is one of your research interests. Having research interests in the first place emphasizes that you do more than just write papers for class—you think about and research topics on your own as well, as Kennedy does.

**Paragraph 2: About Your Article**    The second paragraph must convince the editor to publish your article. You make the case for publication by showing that you are familiar with the content of the journal and that your article is a good match for that content. Kennedy makes this case with the first sentence of his letter:

> The *Minerva Undergraduate Law Review* is the perfect place to publish "'Unequal Laws'" as the article directly addresses the issues of student judicial proceedings and their intersection with criminal and civil law.

Kennedy emphasizes that his topic would be of interest to undergraduates—the primary audience of an undergraduate law journal. He also implies that his topic, student judicial proceedings, is one that students will want to learn more about. Thus, in the second paragraph you should provide a short summary of your article, indicate your familiarity with the journal, and describe who the audience of your piece would be. Tell the editor who would be interested in your article, and why.

**Paragraph 3: Business Details**    The third paragraph thanks the editor for considering your article and tells the editor how to reach you. You can provide more pertinent details about your article here. You should also mention that you welcome editorial suggestions. Editors read many, many articles and they have great expertise. You should express gratitude that they have taken the time to make suggestions to improve your article.

## Submitting to Journals via Email

Many journals now prefer to receive submission via email. When submitting to a journal by email, keep professionalism in mind. This email is the first impression that the journal editors will have of you as a researcher and writer. Here are a few rules of thumb. (Remember, if the journal's guidelines say something different than what is written here, *follow the journal's guidelines.*)

**Abstract**    If your journal does not ask for an abstract, send it anyway. Sometimes journal editors just presume that you will send an abstract as a part of your research.

**Cover Letter**    Paste your cover letter in the body of the email, with one change in formatting. Instead of putting your contact information first, *move it to the bottom of the letter, after your name.* The address of the editor will be first, then the body of the letter, then your name and address. This is the standard format for professional email correspondence.

You can also create a professional email signature with your contact information that your email software will automatically append to the bottom of all of the emails that you compose.

**Document Filenames**    Name your documents in a useful way: lastname_abstract.doc or lastname_articletitle.doc. You must put your last name in the document's filename because editors receive hundreds of documents called "abstract.doc" and "article.doc." The courteous and professional move is to name your documents in a useful manner. Use .doc and *not* .docx format (the format of the newest version of Microsoft Word) because many computers cannot read .docx format. You can change the format of your document by selecting "Save As" and then selecting ".doc" from the drop-down menu.

**Font**    Use a common font in your article. Common fonts are available across many operating systems and word processors. The default fonts of many word processors, especially the latest version of Microsoft Office, are neither common nor universally available across different computers. You want your document to appear the same on your editor's computer as it does on yours; therefore, you should use a common font. Common fonts include the following: Times New Roman, Courier New, Georgia, Arial, and Verdana.

**Email Subject Line**    The subject line of your email should read "Article Submission." You can also put your last name and the title of your document, but "Article Submission" should come first.

You have now completed a difficult journey, from learning the legal system to learning to read a case, from brainstorming your research topic to completing your research and writing an outline, from drafting and revising a research paper to submitting that paper for publication in a scholarly journal. You should be proud of yourself.

# Appendix A

## Glossary of Terms

**Abstract:** A short document that summarizes the arguments, findings, and conclusions of a scholarly article.

**Administrative Regulations:** Rules passed by government agencies.

***Amicus* Brief:** A brief filed by a "friend of the court" in hopes of influencing the court's opinion.

**Analogize:** To argue that an earlier case is similar to the case at hand, and therefore the case at hand should have the same outcome as the earlier case. Compare with "Distinguish."

**Anglo-American Legal System:** The legal system that began in the middle ages in England and is now shared by some former British colonies, including the United States.

**Appeal:** To challenge a lower court's ruling in a higher court.

**Appellant:** The party who files in appeal in a case.

**Appellate Brief:** Document written for the court by an appealing party setting out the arguments for the appeal.

**Authority:** Primary and secondary sources and other types of evidence used in legal writing.

**Bluebook:** The style of legal citation used by legal professionals and law reviews.

**Boolean Operators:** In digital research, search terms used to limit a keyword search.

**C-RAC:** The basic framework of legal analysis; an acronym for conclusion, rule, analysis, conclusion.

**Case:** Any conflict between two or more parties that has entered the legal system.

**Case Brief:** An outline of the important parts of an appellate court opinion.

**Case Citation:** A series of numbers and letters that indicates where an opinion is published.

**Case Law:** Law made through individual cases decided by judges. Part of the common law.

**Case Name:** The title of a legal case composed of the names of the parties separated by a "v."

**Ceremonial Oratory:** A genre of oratory used to praise a person or to blame a person for wrongdoing. Also called "Epideictic" oratory.

**Citation:** A reference to an external source.

**Citation Signal:** A word or phrase that indicates that the writer is about to quote, paraphrase, or summarize source material.

**Citation Style:** A system used by writers to communicate with readers the sources used in a piece of writing.

**Cliché:** A phrase that has been overused to the point that it has lost its original meaning.

**Common Law:** The common law uses previously decided cases to determine what the law is in a current case.

**Concurring Opinion:** A judicial opinion written by the judges who agree with the holding of the majority but disagree with the majority's reasoning. Has no legal force. Sometimes called a "concurrence."

**Confirmation:** In classical rhetoric, the proof of a speech composed of supporting arguments and evidence.

**Controlling Precedent:** Precedent that a court must follow when making decisions because it was created by courts in its path of appeal.

**Counterargument:** Any possible argument that opposes your thesis or supporting arguments and requires you to make a rebuttal. See "Rebuttal."

**Court of Appeals:** A higher court composed of judges who review what happened during at trial or at a hearing of a lower court of appeals. The U.S. Supreme Court is the highest court of appeals in the United States.

**Dissenting Opinion:** A judicial opinion written by the judges who disagree with the majority of the court. Has no legal force. Sometimes called a "dissent."

**Distinguish:** To point out differences between an earlier case and a case at hand in order to argue that the earlier case should not affect the present case's outcome. Compare with "Analogize."

**Docket Number:** A number assigned by a court to identify a case.

**Enthymeme:** A type of syllogism in which a premise, usually the major premise, is left unspoken or unwritten.

**Executive Order:** An order issued by the U.S. president, having the force of law so long as its contents lie within the discretion of the president.

**Exordium:** In classical rhetoric, the introductory portion of a speech.

**Federal Statute:** Laws passed by both houses of the U.S. Congress and signed by the president.

**Forensic Oratory:** A genre of classical oratory that seeks to discover the truth about the past. Sometimes called "legal" or "judicial" oratory.

**Genre:** A type of document designed to accomplish certain purposes (e.g., a court opinion, an *amicus* brief). Therefore, documents within a genre share a specific set of conventions.

**Government Printing Office:** Agency of the legislative branch that publishes legislative, judicial, and executive documents.

**Hanging Indent:** An element of a page format in which the first line of every paragraph is flush to the left margin while every line of the paragraph thereafter is indented by half an inch.

**Holding:** In a judicial opinion, a clear statement of the case's legal effect. Also called a "ruling."

**Hyperbole:** When a writer or speaker exaggerates a position in order to create strong emotional responses in an audience.

**Issue:** The legal question an appeals court must decide, also called the "question presented." A part of a case brief.

**Judicial Review:** The power held by U.S. courts to say whether legislation violates the Constitution.

**Jurisdiction:** A court's legal authority or power over the issues of a case.

***Kairos*:** Ancient Greek term for "time"; refers to timeliness, a specific point in time, rather than to chronological time. A rhetorical term.

**Legal *Topoi*:** Categories of common arguments used by judges, legal scholars, and lawyers.

**Legal Writing:** The skill of making legal claims and supporting them with authority.

**Legalese:** The legal jargon and syntax that often clogs and confuses legal documents.

**Legislation:** Laws made by any governing body or legislature. Sometimes called "statutes."

**Legislative Intent:** A theory of statutory interpretation that looks to the intent, or purpose, of the legislative body that enacted the statute.

**Metadiscourse:** Places in a text where the author refers to the text itself rather than the topic of the text.

**Methodology:** In a research paper, a brief overview of how the author will prove a thesis; a step-by-step description of the paper's supporting arguments.

**Moot:** When a conflict has already been resolved or somehow placed beyond the reach of the law.

**Morals:** Community-driven rules created by a group of people to govern their collective behavior.

**Narration:** In classical rhetoric, the portion of a speech that provides background information.

**Nominalized Verb:** A verb construction that transforms a verb into a noun, paired with some form of the verb "to be."

**Opinion:** A document written by one or more judges of a court in which they analyze the issues of the case and provide a holding.

**Oral Argument:** A formal discussion between the judges of an appeals court and the lawyers of the parties on appeal, in which they review the arguments at issue.

**Ordinance:** Law passed by city and country governments.

**Overturn:** When the Supreme Court declares one of its earlier rulings incorrect. Same as "overrule."

**Page Break:** An invisible marker in a word processor document that tells a printer to end a page where the marker is inserted rather than at the end of the actual sheet of paper. Useful between the end of a paper and the beginning of a bibliography.

**Paired Synonyms:** A verbal quirk of legal writing that occurs when two words that mean the same thing are put together and joined by "and."

**Paraphrase:** Restating the thoughts or ideas of another using a similar number of words.

**Partition:** In classical rhetoric, the portion of a speech that divides the speech into manageable parts.

**Passive Verb:** A verbal construction that combines the past participle of a verb with some form of the verb "to be."

**Path of Appeal:** The courts to which parties can appeal a decision of a lower court. In the U.S. federal system, a trial verdict can be appealed to one of the U. S.Circuit Courts of Appeal and then to the U.S. Supreme Court.

**Peroration:** In classical rhetoric, the conclusion portion of a speech.

**Persuasive Precedent:** Precedent that a court may choose to take into consideration but is not required to follow, including decisions by lower courts and courts in other jurisdictions.

**Petition for Appeal:** A document filed by a lawyer on behalf of a client who wishes to appeal a lower court ruling. See also "Appeal."

**Petitioner:** The appellant in a Supreme Court case, so called because one must first petition the Supreme Court to hear an appeal. Sometimes called "appellant."

**Plagiarism:** Using another person's words or ideas and claiming them as one's own.

**Plain English Movement:** A movement within government and law to remove complex language from government documents and to write in language that an average reader can understand.

**Plain Meaning:** A theory of statutory interpretation that states that the ordinary meaning of the words of a statute should control the interpretation.

**Political Oratory:** A genre of oratory used to discover the best way to resolve a current conflict. Associated with government officials.

**Primary Source:** First-hand testimony, documents, letters, diaries and other materials that make up the object of research.

**Procedural History:** A description of how a case has progressed through the court system.

**Public Policy:** The decisions a government makes regarding certain conflicts and the effects these decisions have on the public.

**Rebuttal:** Response to a counterargument. See "Counterargument."

**Refutation:** In classical rhetoric, the portion of a speech in which the speaker presents counterarguments and refutes them.

**Reporters:** Books in which judicial opinions are published.

**Respondent:** On appeal to the U.S. Supreme Court, the party responding to the appeal. Sometimes called "appellee."

**Revision:** An in-depth rethinking of every part of a writing project.

**Rhetoric:** The ability to identify and use the appropriate means of persuasion in any given situation.

**Rhetorical Analysis:** An examination of the types and quality of the arguments made in a piece of communication.

**Rhetorical Appeals:** Categories of the different ways that speakers make arguments. Developed by Aristotle, who named them *"ethos," "logos,"* and *"pathos."* Also called rhetorical "proofs."

**Rhetorical Fallacy:** A syllogism, or argument, whose logic fails or whose premises are untrue. Fallacies can be "formal" or "informal."

**Rhetorical Question:** A question whose answer is implied by the way it is asked or framed.

**Roadmap:** A rhetorical arrangement tool used when giving oral presentations, which provides a list of the contents of the presentation to come. Often used with "signposts" to guide an audience through a speech.

**Ruling:** In a judicial opinion, a clear statement of the case's legal effect. Also called a "holding."

**Scholarly Conference:** A gathering of scholars who share an interest in a certain field in order to present recent research.

**Scholarly Conversation:** Ideas that scholars have already written about your topic and the current scholarly debates on your topic. Also called "scholarly context."

**Secondary Source:** Any text written about the object of study. Usually written by a scholar in the field. Compare with "Primary Source."

**Signpost:** A metadiscursive sentence that guides a reader through an article.

**Sophists:** Rhetoric teachers of ancient Athens who trained citizens to argue cases in court.

***Stare Decisis:*** Literally, "let the decision stand." The doctrine holds that courts should follow the law set forth in prior cases.

***Statutes at Large:*** Annual publication of laws passed by Congress, published by the Government Printing Office. See also *"United States Code."*

**Summary:** Restatement of the thoughts or ideas of another in a form much shorter than the original.

**Thesis:** In scholarly writing, the main argument of an article, which can be summarized in one sentence.

**Treaty:** An international agreement between two or more nations.

**Trial Transcript:** The precise record of every word spoken at trial. Formatted like a script.

**Unconstitutional:** In violation of a constitution. Usually refers to a rule or regulation.

***United States Code:*** Republished every six years, the formal codification of all federal laws into fifty sections, called "titles."

**Writ of Certiorari:** A special petition for appeal filed with the U.S. Supreme Court.

**Writer's Guidelines:** The rules that authors must follow when they submit an article to a journal. Each journal has guidelines that an author must follow.

**Writing Workshop:** A group of friends or colleagues who meet to read and comment on each other's writing in order to improve their work.

# *Appendix B*

## Sample Student Writing

In this appendix, you will find samples of the types of writing discussed in this book, written by real undergraduate students. The genres are divided into two groups: writing about cases, which includes rhetorical analyses and case briefs, and scholarly legal writing.

## WRITING ABOUT CASES

### Rhetorical Analysis

#### Kennedy's Opinion: Effective for His Purpose?

In the Supreme Court case of *Lawrence v. Texas*, Justice Anthony Kennedy delivers the opinion of the Court. Kennedy forcefully and repeatedly sets forth the liberties that he believes should be granted to every American. Kennedy establishes himself as an authority on this case by demonstrating his knowledge of previous, pertinent cases and of the Constitution. He establishes well-defined boundaries for this ruling, taking into consideration future decisions that will rely upon this case as precedent. By establishing his authority and acknowledging his audiences, Kennedy fulfills his purpose of defending the claim that the Due Process Clause of the Fourteenth Amendment guarantees individuals the right to have private intimate contact without the fear of criminal prosecution.

**Speaker/Ethos**  Justice Kennedy delivers the decision of the court. Justice O'Connor wrote a concurring opinion and Justice Scalia wrote a dissenting opinion. Kennedy and Scalia also wrote on behalf of other justices (Kennedy for the majority, including four other justices, and Scalia for two other dissenting justices). In any Supreme Court opinion, there are implied speakers as well: the U.S. Supreme Court, and, in turn, the U.S. government, of which the Supreme Court is an arm. The president selects and the Senate confirms the Supreme Court justices. Since U.S. voters elect the president and Senate members, Kennedy's opinion also speaks for voting U.S. citizens.

The fact that Kennedy is a Supreme Court Justice gives him an aura of prestige and reliability. Supreme Court justices are known for their legal prowess and their aptitude for interpreting the law. Kennedy demonstrates his knowledge by citing prior cases and Constitutional amendments that pertain to privacy rights. Kennedy's references to cases that concern various aspects of personal liberties show that he is well versed in the law and demonstrate his logical thought process. This combination of legal proficiency and a coherent approach confirms that Kennedy is credible.

Kennedy was appointed to the court by Republican president Ronald Reagan in 1988 and is considered by most legal scholars to be a politically conservative justice. In other cases before the court, he has often voted in agreement with other politically conservative justices, such as former Chief Justice Rehnquist and Associate Justices Scalia, and Thomas—all three of whom dissented in *Lawrence*. Of the five justices who composed the majority in *Lawrence*, then, Kennedy was the most politically conservative. As a Republican appointee and a political conservative, his vote for homosexual rights does not appear to be politically motivated but instead appears driven by justice. Kennedy establishes this politically neutral *ethos* when he writes "The instant case involves liberty of the person both in its spatial and in its more transcendent dimensions" (562). Kennedy insists that "liberty," not partisan politics, drives his opinion.

Kennedy shows himself to be knowledgeable and passionate about the liberties that he states should be granted under the Fourteenth Amendment. He believes that liberty should "[include] freedom of thought, belief, expression, and certain intimate conduct" (562). Kennedy's strong views about certain freedoms allow him to successfully convince his audience that there are aspects of American's lives that should be barred from governmental interference.

**Audience/Pathos**   The legal community, the public, and the press are intended audiences for the opinion of the Court. This opinion informs the public that they, like the petitioners, "are entitled to respect for their private lives" (578). Kennedy considers this audience by precisely stating the rights that this case grants to Americans. To avoid confusion or extrapolation from the decision of this case, Kennedy also clearly states the areas of law that the case does not address. Future courts with similar cases are another audience that Kennedy considers. Since the majority opinion of the Supreme Court is used as a precedent for other cases, there must be clear guidelines and reasoning behind the decision. Therefore, Kennedy sets forth the exact purpose of this case as well as what the case "does not involve" (578).

In the first paragraph of the opinion, Kennedy makes an appeal to *pathos*: "Liberty protects the person from unwarranted government intrusions into a dwelling or other private places. In our tradition the State is not omnipresent in the home" (562). In this paragraph, "liberty" refers to a concept that Americans hold dear, what we often call *freedom*. Kennedy also mentions the "home," invoking the protective feeling most of have toward our living places. Kennedy thus begins his opinion by calling on our shared emotional attachment to freedom and the sanctity of the home. Kennedy appeals again to *pathos* when he writes "When sexuality finds overt expression in intimate conduct with another person, the conduct can be but one element in a personal bond that is more enduring. The liberty protected by the Constitution allows homosexual persons the right to make this choice" (567). Here, he appeals to our common experiences of human emotional and physical bonding, thus arguing that homosexuals should have the freedom to love and touch one another just as heterosexuals do.

Kennedy knows that the American public values privacy; he appeals to this value by using the term "liberty" multiple times. He contends that the decision turns on whether the government can intrude into very private aspects of one's life. He also appeals to the values of love and interpersonal relationships. Therefore, Kennedy defends the court's ruling by stating that intimate "conduct can be but one element in a personal bond that is more enduring" (567).

**Message/Logos**    Kennedy's opinion announces the decision of the Court and provides the reasoning behind that decision. Because *Lawrence* overturns *Bowers v. Hardwick* (1986), Kennedy must convince his audience that *Bowers* relied upon faulty reasoning and did not adhere to the Fourteenth Amendment of the Constitution. In making this argument, he stresses the right of personal liberty for the private and consensual sexual practices of homosexuals. Kennedy specifies that that the decision of this case was reached because the government should not "control a personal relationship" through monitoring of "intimate conduct" (567).

Kennedy appeals to *logos* when he points to earlier cases such as *Griswold v. Connecticut* (1965), *Eisenstadt v. Baird* (1972), and *Roe v. Wade* (1973), claiming that these powerful Supreme Court opinions support the majority holding in *Lawrence*. Few would argue that adults do not have the freedom to use birth control, as established by *Griswold* and *Eisenstadt*. By claiming that the right at stake in *Lawrence* is similar to those of earlier cases, Kennedy builds a logical foundation based on case law. Kennedy's use of these earlier opinions aid his defense of the Court's decision by showing that the outcome has reliable origins.

## Case Brief

### *Lawrence v. Texas*, 539 U.S. 558 (2003)

**Issue:** Does the Texas crime-against-nature statute violate the Due Process Clause of the Fourteenth Amendment to the U.S. Constitution?

**Facts:** Defendants, two men, were arrested in their home for having sex in violation of the Texas crime-against-nature statute. The statute forbids "deviate sexual intercourse" between people of the same sex. The defendants were convicted and fined. They appealed their arrest and conviction through the Texas courts. The U.S. Supreme Court granted their petition for appeal.

**Holding:** Yes, the Texas crime against-nature-statute violates the Due Process Clause of the Fourteenth Amendment to the U.S. Constitution.

**Reasoning:** The majority relies on precedent composed of due process right-to-privacy cases. They start with *Griswold v. CT*, then *Eisenstadt v. Baird*, and then *Roe v. Wade*. They then use this precedent, and the facts of the current case, to overturn *Bowers v. Hardwick*, a 1986 case that upheld a similar sodomy law in Georgia. The court's reliance on *Roe* seems less persuasive than the other cases it uses because *Roe* stands on shaky ground today.

The court makes ethical arguments when it argues that homosexuals, like heterosexuals, should have a right to private sexual relationships. However, this moral argument would be stronger if they addressed the competing moral claims in this case—the right to love and relationships on one hand versus the "traditional" morals that many Americans believe in on the other hand.

The court addresses historical arguments when it claims that "there is no longstanding history" of laws targeting homosexuals (568). They argue that laws forbidding sodomy were directed at heterosexual couples as well, and that it was not until the 1970s that laws targeting homosexuals first appeared. With this argument they seek to debunk the argument in *Bowers* that sodomy laws are deeply rooted in U.S. history. Their separation of sodomy laws from laws targeting homosexuals is accurate but feels unpersuasive. The fact is, like slavery and sexism, sodomy laws have indeed been around for a long time. They did not have to debunk the historical argument in order to declare them unconstitutional.

The court brings in international law when it examines the European court's rulings on sodomy laws (576). The strong stance that Europe has taken against homophobic laws is persuasive to the extent that we care about what our peer nations are doing. Some judges care (like Kennedy) and some do not (like Scalia).

**Concurrence:**  Justice O'Connor agrees that the Texas statute is unconstitutional but disagrees that it violates due process. She argues that because the statute targets homosexuals specifically, it violates equal protection. She also believes that *Bowers* should be overturned.

**Dissent:**  Scalia argues that legislatures should be allowed to make laws based on morals. He also argues that *Bowers* should not have been overturned because overturning the case creates inconsistency in the court's rulings.

# SCHOLARLY LEGAL WRITING

Throughout this book you have become familiar with the work of two student writers, Kennedy and Rachel. As you might remember, Kennedy wrote about student judicial proceedings and Rachel about virtual child pornography. In this Appendix, you will see more writing by these two students. You will also find the work of a third student, Josie, who has written about securities fraud litigation.

## Abstracts

**Title:**  "Virtual Child Pornography: When PROTECTing Children Becomes a Constitutional Question"

**Author:**  Rachel

**Abstract:**  Virtual child pornography—pornographic images of children created with computer software instead of live children—has lately arisen as a free speech debate. Because virtual child pornography looks identical to real child pornography, Congress included prohibitions against it in the PROTECT Act of 2003. The constitutionality of the PROTECT Act has already been challenged in the U.S. Supreme Court, and it is likely to be challenged again because of its controversial nature. I argue that because the Courts have allowed the categorizing of real child pornography as unprotected speech, prohibitions against virtual child pornography are also valid under the Constitution. Accordingly, I first I examine several Supreme Court cases, most notably *Osborne v. Ohio* (1990) and *U.S. v. Nolan* (1987), as evidence that child pornography harms all children, even those not involved in the image production. I then present a psychological study of the effects on adults of viewing virtual child pornography. I read this evidence with the ideas of noted feminist Catherine MacKinnon and show that there is ample evidence of the government's compelling interest to classify virtual child pornography as unprotected speech.

**Title:**    *Stoneridge* and Securities Fraud Litigation: Interpreting Section 10(b) in Light of Crisis in the U.S. Securities Market

**Author:**    Josie James

**Abstract:**    As a byproduct of bailouts and bankruptcies, the Securities Exchange Commission (SEC) has discovered thousands of fraud violations. *Stoneridge Investment Partners, LLC v. Scientific Atlanta, Inc.* (2008) affects this fraud litigation by limiting the liability of secondary agents to fraud. Scholars who support the Supreme Court's decision suggest it prevents unmerited lawsuits. Others suggest *Stoneridge* limits investors' ability to challenge collusive schemes, and I agree. In this paper, I argue that the Supreme Court's decision in *Stoneridge* unreasonably limits the ability of private parties to check fraudulent investment companies and gives too much responsibility to government agencies. Accordingly, I first explore how private enforcement of SEC regulations is crucial to a productive market. Next, I show that the Court's interpretation of section 10(b) lacks clarity. Finally, I show the ways that *Stoneridge* favors corporations and point to the danger this poses in light of recent financial scandals. By focusing on liability instead of guilt, *Stoneridge* makes companies less concerned about the integrity of associates. By limiting liability, *Stoneridge* removes power from investors and makes it easier for companies to engage in fraud.

## Argument Outline

Here is Josie's argument outline. Notice how much detail she provides in this outline and how many specific sources she lists. All of this early work made drafting her paper much easier. At the beginning of her outline, she provides the title of her project and her thesis statement.

She writes her arguments, counterarguments, and rebuttals as complete sentences. Later, she can use these sentences in her final draft if she wishes. Her arguments are well organized, numbered neatly with supporting arguments listed by letter under the main argument they support. Each argument or supporting argument is paired with authority.

For each source she lists, she provides the full works-cited entry in MLA style. In that way, she could always find a source again if she needed to, and when she needed to write her works-cited page, she could just cut and paste from her outline. The first time she mentions a source in the outline, she indicates it in parentheses. At every other mention of the source, she uses an abbreviation to refer to the source.

**Author:**  Josie James

**Argument Outline:**  *Stoneridge* and Securities Fraud Litigation: Interpreting Section 10(b) in Light of Crisis in the U.S. Securities Market

**Thesis:**  In this paper, I argue that the Supreme Court's decision in *Stoneridge Investment Partners v. Scientific-Atlanta* unjustly limits the power of the private parties to check fraudulent investment companies while placing too much responsibility and power in the hands of government agencies.

## 1. Private enforcement is essential to a productive market.

1-A. Counter Argument: Private parties having the ability to sue secondary actors connected to frauds will lead to fears of unwarranted lawsuits, and will cause companies and investors to choose foreign securities markets over U.S. securities markets.

Authority:

Rose, Amanda M. "Reforming Securities Litigation Reform: Restructuring the Relationship Between Public and Private Enforcement of Rule 10B-5." *Columbia Law Review* 108.6 (2008): 1301-1364. JSTOR. Web. 1 March 2010. [First mention of source.]

Rose argues that Rule 10b-5 is overbroad. She argues for a move towards public enforcement by the SEC. She says many scholars believe Rule 10b-5 might result unwarranted class action lawsuits.

1-B. Rebuttal: Others argue that private enforcement results in market transparency and efficiency and actually encourages international and domestic parties to enter the U.S. securities market.

Authority:

Gomm, Seth S. "See No Evil, Hear No Evil, Speak No Evil: *Stoneridge Investment Partners, LLC v. Scientific-Atlanta, Inc.* and the Supreme Court's Attempt to Determine the Issue of Scheme Liability." *Arkansas Law Review* 61.3 (2009): 453-486. Print. [First mention of source.]

Gomm explains the relationship between *Stoneridge* and the SEC and shows how limiting the power of private parties might negatively impact financial markets while outlining the benefits of market transparency.

Primary Sources:

Sarbanes-Oxley Act. Pub L. 107-204. 30 Jul 2002. 116 Stat.745. GPOAccess.gov. Web. 1 March 2010. Available at: <http://frwebgate. access.gpo.gov/cgi-bin/getdoc.cgi?dbname=107_cong_bills&docid=f: h3763enr.tst.pdf>

Securities Exchange Act. Pub. L. 48. 6 June 1934. 48 Stat. 881. 19 Feb. 2009. Securities Lawyer's Deskbook. University of Cincinnati College of Law. Web. 1 March 2010. Available at: <http://www.law.uc. edu/CCL/34Act/>.

These two acts define the need for transparency in U.S. markets.

Transition: By favoring businesses over private parties, *Stoneridge* largely disabled private parties from serving as watchdogs for secondary actors engaged in fraud. Not only did the decision eliminate this method of market regulation, it also failed to install a workable alternative in its place.

## 2. The *Stoneridge* holding is too vague to be effective.   2-A.
Courts do not have a streamlined process for dealing with securities fraud; currently, there is a circuit split.

2-B. The wording of the Court's opinion leaves too much undefined and unaddressed, forcing lower courts to fill in too many blanks.

Evidence: Compare *Stoneridge* to other fraud causes where gaps in the courts' reasoning and rulings caused confusion supports both these points.

Cases to compare:

Central Bank, N.A. v. First Interstate Bank, N.A. 511 U.S. 164. U.S. Supreme Ct. 1994; Simpson v. AOL Time Warner Inc. 452 F.3d 1040. U.S. Ct. of Appeals for the Ninth Circuit. 2006; Blue Chip Stamps v. Manor Drugs Stores. 421 U.S. 723. U.S. Supreme Ct. 1975.

2-C. *Stoneridge* has already been altered by many subsequent cases. Examining their holdings demonstrates some of the hazy areas of the *Stoneridge* ruling.

Evidence from cases altering *Stoneridge* ruling: SEC v. Tambone, 550 F. 3d 106. U.S. Ct. of Appeals for the First Circuit. 2008 (*Stoneridge* cited in dissenting opinion); In re Parmalat Sec. Litig. __F. Supp. 2d__. U.S. Dist. LEXIS 6329. U.S. Dist. Ct. for the Second Circuit. 2009. (Decision contrast to *Stoneridge*); In re Bristol Myers Squibb Co. Sec. Litig. 586 F. Supp. 2d 148. U.S. District Ct. for the Second Circuit 2008.; Marini v. Janus Inv. Fund. U.S. Dist. LEXIS 106333. U.S. Dist Ct. for the Fourth Circuit. 2008.; SEC v. Bolla. 550 F. Supp. 2d 54. U.S. Dist. Ct. for the D.C. Circuit. 2008.

2-D. Debate exists over whether *Stoneridge* place more power in the hands of the investors or less power in the hands of the investors.

Authority: Rose, Amanda M. "Reforming Securities Litigation Reform." Rose argues more power will be given to private parties as a result of *Stoneridge*. Gomm and Prentice both suggest *Stoneridge* gives less power to private investors, but I want to keep looking for an alternative source that more clearly outlines this point.

Transition: Less power is being placed in the hands of the investors because of the way the Court interpreted section 10(b) and Rule 10b-5.

### 3. The Court's interpretation of section 10(b) and Rule 10b-5 conflicted with existing legal precedent (Legal precedent). 3-A. Lower courts had systems that provided guidelines for when secondary violators could be tried as primary violators: Bright Line Test, Substantial Participation test, Primary Liability and Secondary Liability and their relationship to Scheme Liability.

Authority:

Souza, Travis S. "Freedom to Defraud: *Stoneridge*, Primary Liability, and the Need to Properly Define Section 10(B)." *Duke Law Journal* 57.4 (2008): 1179-1207. Print. (First mention of source.)

Travis Souza outlines these different tests and shows their connection to *Stoneridge*.

Primary Authority: Simpson v. AOL Time Warner, Inc. 452 F3d 1040. US. Ct. of Appeals for the Ninth Circuit. 2006. This case is an example of Substantial Participation.

Transition: The precedent set by these lower courts was closer to the legislative intent of section 10(b) and Rule 10b-5.

### 4. The Court's interpretation of section 10(b) and Rule 10b-5 was a stark departure from the legislative intent of these codes. 4-A. The intent was to provide means of conviction for all guilty parties, no matter who the accuser.

Authority: Souza, Travis S. "Freedom to Defraud." Souza says the Court departed from the legislative intent of section 10(b).

4-B. The Court ignored the wording of section 10(b) in favor of an interpretation that defied many existing forms of legislation.

Authority:

Prentice, Robert A. "*Stoneridge*, Securities Fraud Litigation, and the Supreme Court." *American Business Law Journal* 45.4 (2008): 611-683. (First mention of source.)

Prentice says the Court overstepped its bounds by limiting freedoms that have been in place for dozens of years.

4-C. Counter-Argument: Both Rule 10-b5 and section 10(b) are written as guidelines for the SEC, not the general public.

Authority: Rose, Amanda M. "Reforming Securities Litigation Reform." Rose says the scope of Rule 10b-5 is limited to the SEC.

4-D. Rebuttal: It outlines what is illegal and has been used as precedent by judges in courts, thus it should extend as a precedent that can be used by the people.

Authority: Rule 10b-5 and section 10(b) have been cited in the Court's reasoning in every case mentioned thus far (see cases listed above).

Transition: There is an inherent paradox in acknowledging that the actions of Motorola and Scientific-Atlanta were deceptive but saying that they failed to meet the standards of section 10(b).

### 5. The Court's interpretation of section 10(b) was unethical.

5-A. Motorola and Scientific-Atlanta clearly knew they were engaging in deceptive acts, and the Court recognized this argument as well.

Primary Authority: Stoneridge Inv. Partners. LLC. v. Scientific-Atlanta, Inc. Oral Argument. 552 U.S. ___ . 128 S. Ct. 761. U.S. Supreme Ct. 2008. 24 Feb. 2009. Available at: http://www.oyez.org/cases/2000-2009/2007/2007_06_43/argument/.

5-B. Their interpretation of reliance in relation to section 10(b) was overly strict. Definition of reliance was met.

Authority: Gomm, "See No Evil." Gomm says the reliance precedent was met in this case, but that the Supreme Court inflated it in order to make their ruling; Souza, "Freedom to Defraud." Souza claims the Court misinterpreted the intent of section 10(b).

Transition: The *Stoneridge* holding sets unethical precedent. The opinion issued by the Court implies that as long as companies do not disclose their sham transactions to the public, they aren't liable.

Authority: Gomm, Seth S. "See No Evil." Gomm shows the thwarted logic in allowing a company to engage in fraud so long as they do not make it known.

### 6. The precedent set by *Stoneridge* (and *Central Bank*) is unclear and easily manipulated by parties guilty of fraudulent activities. (Ethics, History, Societal Consensus)

6-A. The Court's holding created legal loopholes that favor corporations. "The Narrowing Approach": There are problems using judicial rulings as guidelines for market behavior.

Authority: Rose, "Reforming Securities Litigation Reform." Rose says that a by-product of the current treatment of section 10(b) is that courts are creating legal loopholes and precedent that is constantly changing.

6-B. It appears as though the Court made their decision based on which side they wanted lower courts to favor.

Authority:

Chrisman, Rodney D. "*Stoneridge v. Scientific-Atlanta*: Do Section 10(B) and Rule 10B-5 Require a Misstatement or Omission?" *QLR* 26.4 (2008): 839-918. Print. [First mention of source.]

Chrisman argues the Court made their decision based off policy considerations.

6-B. The actions of Motorola, Charter, and Scientific-Atlanta, especially in regards to their communications with the public, are in many ways parallel to the actions resulting in the recent scandals/bankruptcies of companies like AIG, Bear Sterns, Lehman Brothers, and more.

Authority: Gomm, Seth S. "See No Evil." Gomm outlines the types of transactions that could be considered fraudulent and subject to scheme liability. Gomm also points to evidence in the transcript, asking if there should be a difference between "the realm of financing business" and "the realm of ordinary business operations."

Primary Authority: Stoneridge Inv. Partners. LLC. v. Scientific-Atlanta, Inc. 552 U.S. ___ . 128 S. Ct. 761. U.S. Supreme Ct. 2008. 24 Feb. 2009. This Opinion outlines how companies engaged in deceptive practices.

## Research Paper

Here is Josie's finished research paper. If you would like to see another sample paper, much of Rachel's paper appears in Chapter 5.

If you read her argument outline as just given, then you are already familiar with much of the content of Josie's paper. You can see how she transitions from a highly organized outline into a similarly well organized research paper.

Josie does many things right in this paper. Pay attention to her strong signposts and topic sentences. Notice how well she integrates sources into her text; you always know who is "talking" in her paragraphs. Even if you do not know much about securities regulation, Josie's background paragraphs provide enough information that you can follow her arguments.

Josie James

Professor Pryal

English 305, Section 1

March 5, 2010

*Stoneridge* and Securities Fraud Litigation:

Interpreting Section 10(b) in light of Crisis

in the U.S. Securities Market

As a result of billion dollar bailouts, bankruptcies, and men like Bernard Madoff, Congress
and the Securities Exchange Commission (SEC) are
currently dealing with hundreds of fraud violations. Many investors, businesses, charities, and
endowments have lost the bulk of their assets.
With injured parties seeking redress for losses in
light of corporate scandals, the precedent for
securities fraud litigation set by the Supreme
Court in *Stoneridge Investment Partners, LLC v.
Scientific Atlanta, Inc.* (2008) has newfound importance. Business and legal scholars who support the
Court's decision in *Stoneridge*, which limits the

ability of private citizens to sue secondary

actors to fraud, say it will prevent unmerited

lawsuits and increase confidence and participation

in U.S. securities markets. On the other hand,

scholars who oppose the decision argue that it

will inhibit market growth by taking away rights

of private investors to confront companies that

have mismanaged their assets. While I agree that

a heyday of unmerited litigation would discourage

companies from participating in U.S. securities

markets, I think sufficient methods for eliminating

such lawsuits are already in place. Furthermore,

I consider it crucial to the success of American

democracy that private individuals have the abil-

ity to challenge all companies who have abused

investors' trust. In this paper, I argue that the

Supreme Court's decision in *Stoneridge* unjustly

limits the power of the private parties to check

fraudulent investment companies and places too

much power in the hands of government agencies.

Giving additional responsibility to the already

full-slated SEC will result in oversights and market deficiencies that will harm investors and increase illegal collusions among companies. To prove this point, I will first show that private enforcement of SEC regulations is crucial to an efficient and productive market. Next, I will show that due to the Court's interpretation of section 10(b), the *Stoneridge* holding lacks clarity as an effective form of market regulation. Finally, I will examine how the Court's decision unduly favors corporations and point to the dangers this favor poses in light of recent financial scandals.

In order to understand how *Stoneridge* has influenced securities fraud litigation, it is first necessary to examine the case and the legislation on which it centered. Stoneridge Investing Partners was the lead plaintiff in a class-action suit filed against Scientific-Atlanta and Motorola, on the grounds that they intentionally schemed with Charter Communications to mislead shareholders by inflating the value of Charter stock for the

2000 fiscal year. Motorola and Scientific-Atlanta allowed Charter to generate the appearance of revenue by selling to Charter cable converter boxes that were overpriced by $20, and agreeing to compensate for the overpayment by purchasing Charter advertising (Stoneridge 766-767). The companies backdated the sale of the boxes to make them appear separate from the purchase of advertising. When Charter filed that year's financial statement with the Securities and Exchange Commission, the company's value was inflated by approximately $17 million (Stoneridge 767). The Supreme Court decided that Motorola and Scientific-Atlanta had too indirect a role to result in harm to investors. In the majority opinion, Justice Kennedy says, "our own determination [is] that the respondents' acts were not relied on by investors and that, as a result, liability cannot be imposed on respondents" (Stoneridge 769). As a result of the holding, investors who purchased Charter stock based on its inflated value could not seek retribution from

Motorola or Scientific-Atlanta. The Court's reasoning was largely based on two pieces of legislation: section 10(b) of the Securities Exchange Act and Rule 10b-5 of the Securities Exchange Commission. According to section 10(b) of the Securities Exchange Act, it is "unlawful for any person, directly or indirectly...[t]o use or employ, in connection with the purchase or sale of any security...any manipulative or deceptive device or contrivance in contravention of such rules and regulations as the Commission may prescribe as necessary." Similarly, SEC Rule 10b-5 makes it illegal to "employ any device, scheme, or artifice to defraud." Later I will examine the Court's interpretation of section 10(b) and Rule 10b-5, but first I want to show why private enforcement of these codes is essential to a healthy market.

As a result of the *Stoneridge* holding, private investors have difficulty challenging accomplices to fraud in a court of law. My own view, however, is that private enforcement of market rules and regulations is essential to a flourishing market. When considering this argument, I think it is first helpful to consider the reasoning of scholars who disapprove of private enforcement. They believe that private parties having the ability to sue companies indirectly involved in fraud leads to fears of unwarranted lawsuits that could effect whole industries and discourage market participation. This is the viewpoint presented by Amanda Rose, an assistant professor of Law at Vanderbilt University. She writes, "Law and economics scholarship teaches that 'bounty hunter' enforcement of an overbroad law, like Rule 10b-5, may lead to overdeterrence and stymie governmental efforts to set effective enforcement policy" (1301). Rose's point is that since Rule 10b-5 can be broadly interpreted, it could likely result in unwarranted class-action suits that would discourage companies from bringing their business to U.S. markets (1301-1302). Though Rose does raise a possible negative consequence of Rule 10b-5, I disagree with her assessment. Scholars who argue that private enforcement is beneficial to U.S. markets have a more solid case. There are two components to this opinion. First, measures to deter unwarranted lawsuits are already in place. One example of such measures is the Private Securities Litigation Reform Act of 1995 (PSLRA). The PSLRA states that "the plaintiff shall have the burden of proving that the act or omission of the defendant alleged to violate this chapter caused the loss" [PSLRA Sec.78u-4(4)]. In other words, the PSLRA states that plaintiffs must have evidence pointing to intended fraud before they can proceed with a lawsuit. Secondly, private enforcement is a necessary supplement to the monitoring processes of the SEC. Seth Gomm, a practicing corporate and securities lawyer and Business Law scholar says, "permitting shareholders to bring private section 10(b) actions against scheming secondary actors would improve the efficiency, transparency, and integrity of the United States securities market. Investors

that are directly victimized by such schemes
should be able to initiate private actions in
order to seek redress for their losses without
having to wait for the SEC to act" (455). In other
words, allowing individual parties to file suit
against fraudulent companies improves the timeliness and accuracy of punishment for those who
violate market regulations. The essence of Gomm's
argument is that because private investors keep
close tabs on companies responsible for their
money, they may pick up on things that the SEC may
miss (455). Stoneridge diminishes the benefits of
private enforcement, since it largely disabled
private parties from serving as watchdogs for secondary actors engaging in fraud. The *Stoneridge*
holding eliminated a crucial method of market regulation and failed to install a working alternative in its place.

*Stoneridge* not only stifles natural market
checks, it also lacks the clarity to effectively
regulate the securities market. *Stoneridge* is not

alone in committing this error. The problem arose
in *Central Bank v. First Interstate Bank* (1994), a
predecessor that ruled against "private civil liability" for aiders and abettors to fraud, claiming
that it was outside the scope of section 10(b)
(Central Bank 177). To examine the failures of
*Stoneridge*, it is first necessary to understand how
*Central Bank* created a lower court divide that
*Stoneridge* needed to resolve. In *Central Bank*, the
Court formed criteria that had to be met in order
for a party to be liable under section 10(b).
Using *Basic Inc. v. Levinson* (1988) as precedent,
the *Central Bank* Court said that a "reliance requirement" had to be met. They held that "a plaintiff in a 10b-5 action must prove that he relied
on the defendant's misinterpretation in order to
recover damages" (Central Bank 178). Though the
ruling was made in part to protect parties who had
unintentionally aided fraud, the Court failed to
adequately outline procedure for cases where second party actors met the reliance requirement or

where the second party actors colluded to engage in fraud, a situation known as scheme liability. I agree with legal scholar Travis Souza that the Court's opinion was too vague. He observes that "it was left to the lower courts to determine when the conduct of an actor qualifies that actor as a primary violator under section 10(b) and Rule 10b-5," and asserts that since *Central Bank*, there have been more cases concerning the definition of primary liability (1182-83). Souza's point is that in the aftermath of *Central Bank*, courts have had to come up with their own methods of distinguishing the difference between primary and secondary liability (1182-83). Their methods range from very broad to extremely narrow. In *Simpson v. AOL Time Warner Inc.* (2006), for example, the Ninth Circuit used scheme liability to hold secondary actors liable if they had substantially participated in the fraudulent act (Simpson 1043). In *Regents of the University of California v. Credit Suisse First Boston* (2007), however, the Fifth Circuit adopted a more narrow definition of primary liability, saying that liability was limited to defendants who made "public and material misrepresentations; i.e., the type of fraud on which an efficient market may be presumed to rely" (Credit Suisse 386-387). The spectrum of interpretations of *Central Bank* is evidence of the confusion it caused. What is more, many scholars feel that *Stoneridge* is currently influencing lower courts in the same way.

Though *Stoneridge* was an opportunity to streamline the procedure for establishing second party fraud liability, it left too many issues unaddressed to accomplish this goal. Like *Central Bank*, it failed to directly address scheme liability (Souza 1194-1199). In U.S. District Court for the Second Circuit, the limited scope of *Stoneridge* has already been questioned. For example, in the case of *In re Parmalat Sec. Litig.* (2008), the Court ignored the precedent set by *Stoneridge* despite the fact that both cases concern Securities Exchange Act violations. District

Judge Lewis A. Kaplan explained, "*Stoneridge* did not deal with the question presented here, viz. whether a principal is liable vicariously for an Exchange Act violation committed by its agent acting within the agent's scope of employment. There are substantial reasons why its holding should not be extended, at least by a district court" (In re Parmalat Sec. Litig. 13). I think this confusion results from the Court's unconventional interpretation of section 10(b), the rule used in all of the cases discussed above. Travis Souza agrees when he writes, "Unfortunately, the Supreme Court appears to have missed the mark. It neglected to recognize that the language of section 10(b) and Rule 10b-5 is vastly different as it pertains to primary liability—especially scheme liability—than it is in relation to aiding and abetting liability" (1206). Souza's assessment points to the fact that *Stoneridge*'s ambiguity on this issue is what makes it an ineffective market regulator.

Now that I have established the inefficiencies that *Stoneridge* has caused in the markets and legal system, I will examine why I believe the Court misinterpreted section 10(b) and Rule 10b-5. By interpreting fraud liability so narrowly, the Court departed from the legislative intent of these codes and the original goal of the Securities Exchange Act of 1934 (Prentice 622-623). The intent of section 10(b) was to provide a means of conviction for all guilty parties, regardless of the accuser. In contrast, the Court's interpretation limits who can qualify as a guilty party and places primary responsibility for identifying these infractions on the SEC. Robert A. Prentice, a professor of Business Law at the University of Texas at Austin, also thinks that the intention of 1934 legislators was to punish anyone who knowingly participated in fraud. Prentice asserts that "it would have been superfluous to have included an express provision imposing a form of aiding and abetting secondary liability when, given the existing state of the law, Congress would have necessarily envisioned that knowing participation in securities fraud would result in joint and several liability" (622-623). The essence of his argument is that the difference between primary and secondary liability is a moot point under the original intent of the law (622-623). Applying this reasoning to *Stoneridge* leaves little doubt that under the original statute, liability would extend to companies colluding to engage in fraud, such as Motorola and Scientific-Atlanta.

Though I agree with Prentice's assessment, it is important to note that the scope of section 10(b) has been narrowed by more recent securities fraud cases, most significantly, *Central Bank*. I argue, however, that even given the narrowed scope of section 10(b), the Court's interpretation was still against legislative intent. As I mentioned earlier, the *Stoneridge* Court declared that the plaintiffs had to meet a reliance requirement in light of the precedent set by *Central Bank*

(Stoneridge 768). The Court felt that Motorola and Scientific-Atlanta were too far removed from investors to be liable, and held that the reliance requirement was not met (Stoneridge 769). Kennedy wrote that they were not liable because "no member of the investing public had knowledge... of the respondents' deceptive acts during relevant times" (Stoneridge 769). I disagree with the Court's conclusion. Regardless of whether investors were aware of Charter's specific transactions with Motorola and Scientific-Atlanta, they still *relied* on the numbers provided by these companies when purchasing stock. Like legal scholar Travis Souza, I feel that the Court inflated the reliance requirement in *Stoneridge* (Souza 1195). According to Souza, "The Court's application of the reliance requirement is flawed. It is widely accepted that reliance is an element brought under section 10(b) to ensure that there is a sufficient causal connection between an actor's conduct and an investor's injury. The Court has never held that an investor must be aware of the specific acts that create the misstatement in order to meet the reliance requirement" (1195). Souza is insisting that the Court defied legal precedent with this interpretation, since there had been many previous cases where the reliance requirement was easier to meet. *Stoneridge* was held to a different, more rigid standard. By giving the plaintiffs in *Stoneridge* this heightened burden of proof, the Court tailored policies to place less power in the hands of investors. This result suggests that the Court's decision was based on predicted impact rather than precedent.

In order to explore this claim, I will now show how the ethicality of the Court's decision is called into question when their reasoning is examined. There is an inherent paradox in acknowledging that the actions of Motorola and Scientific-Atlanta were deceptive but stating that they failed to meet the standards of section 10(b). Motorola and Scientific-Atlanta clearly knew that

they were engaging in deceptive acts, and members
of the Court recognized this argument as well. In
his dissent, Justice Stevens writes of Charter inflating its revenues, "It could not have done so
absent the knowingly fraudulent actions of
Scientific-Atlanta, Inc. and Motorola, Inc.
Investors relied on Charter's revenue statements
in deciding whether to invest in Charter and in
doing so relied on respondents' fraud, which was
itself a 'deceptive device' prohibited by section
10(b) of the Securities Exchange Act of 1934"
(Stoneridge 774). Scholars also contend that the
Court's expansion of the reliance requirement was
unseemly. I agree with Seth Gomm, who extends the
issue of ethicality back to the Court's interpretation of reliance. He asserts, "The result appears to be that, so long as companies *do not disclose* to the public the truth behind sham
contracts and transactions in which they have participated (thereby causing reliance), the companies probably will not be vulnerable to private

actions from shareholders" (455). The opinion issued by the Court implies that as long as companies do not publicize their acts of fraud, they
aren't liable (Gomm 455). It appears that the
Court's decision was based on impact to policy
rather than the facts of the case.

A key problem in *Stoneridge*, and other securities fraud cases, is that the Court's holding
created legal loopholes that favor corporations.
Many scholars fear that parties seeking to engage
in fraudulent activities will manipulate the
*Stoneridge* holding. I agree with Amanda Rose, who
says that there are problems using judicial rulings as guidelines for market behavior. Rose
thinks both underdeterrence and overdeterrence
are problems with section 10(b) liability (1350-
1358). As I stated earlier, I disagree that
overdeterrence is a serious threat of section
10(b); however, I do agree that there is danger
in allowing courts to gerrymander the scope of
10(b). Rose says, "The upshot is that the narrow-

ing approach risks replacing overinclusion with underinclusion. Indeed, it risks creating precisely the 'loopholes' overbroad laws seeks to avoid. Eliminating enterprise liability in private Rule 10b-5 litigation, for example, could ensure that corporations do not excessively invest in precautions to protect against fraud by their agents, but it might also lead to an inadequate investment in precautions" (1353). In other words, companies might not be as careful about examining the integrity of companies with which they choose to interact. This is already a relevant problem; for example, consider AIG choosing to insure companies backing inappropriate numbers of unreliable borrowers with low credit ratings. Not only does the Court's decision create legal loopholes, it also appears as though the Court made their decision based on which side they wanted lower courts to favor. Rodney Chrisman, an assistant professor of Law at Liberty University, says that one reason the decision is so confusing is because the Court made their decision based off predicted impact rather than rhetoric (916). He says, "decisions based upon policy rather than legal argument frequently bring about uncertainty and unintended consequences that inexorably lead to more litigation—arguably, in *Stoneridge*, the very result the Supreme Court seemed so desperate to avoid" (916). Later on, Chrisman says, "While the Court reached what is arguably the right result, it did so in an opinion that is clearly driven by policy considerations more than a careful and thoughtful analysis of the law" (918). Chrisman thinks the Court reached the right decision because he thinks section 10(b) and Rule 10b-5 require a direct misstatement (916-918). I have shown earlier that I disagree with this interpretation, but I do agree that the decision was inappropriately based off policy rather than legal argument. The decision to favor companies is one the Court will soon regret. *Stoneridge* was decided just before the mortgage crisis and the

collapse of dozens of major businesses and banks.
The SEC cannot serve as a lone watchdog since it
has, in recent history, failed to identify many
major fault-lines in the securities industry.

The flaw in *Stoneridge* is that the Court's
focus is on whether the defendants are eligible
for primary liability instead of whether they are
guilty. Like *Central Bank*, *Stoneridge* confuses
lower courts because it departs from the overall
intent of securities fraud litigation—identifying
fraud violations. As Souza emphasizes, "the dri-
ving rationale of securities regulation should be
deterrence, and in the context of section 10(b),
the deterrence purpose should be cabined with
predictability" (1205). In other words, the Court
needs to concentrate on disciplining parties
who commit criminal actions (Souza 1204-1205).
Over the last century, Congress has made several
attempts to protect investors from crooked
companies by enacting legislation such as the
Securities Exchange Act of 1934 and the Sarbanes-

Oxley Act of 2002, which both imposed stricter standards for transparency and accountability on publicly-traded companies. By interpreting section 10(b) so narrowly, however, the Court limited the effect of these efforts. I think the Court will regret its decision as it begins to see the inefficiencies that *Stoneridge* brings to the U.S. securities market. Seth Gomm agrees when he writes, "[a]lthough the current Court is unlikely to allow private scheme-liability actions in the near future, Congress may act in favor of shareholder-plaintiffs when it sees the wisdom of allowing such section 10(b) actions" (454). Gomm's point is that the U.S. securities market will soon feel the effect of the absence of private party plaintiffs, and I agree with this prediction. The actions of Motorola, Charter, and Scientific-Atlanta, especially in regards to their communications with the public, are in many ways parallel to the actions resulting in the recent scandals and failures of companies like

AIG, Bear Sterns, and Lehman Brothers. Checks by individual investors are needed to ensure that these reformulated companies do not continue to engage in reckless market practices. Investors' input is essential to a free, productive market. Scheme liability is one of the major issues facing society today, and *Stoneridge* has set dangerous precedent that removes power from the hands of investors, places additional burdens on the already over-extended SEC, and makes it easier for companies to engage in underhanded schemes that perpetuate deceit and fraud.

## Works Cited

Central Bank, N.A. v. First Interstate Bank, N.A. 511 U.S. 164. U.S. Supreme Ct. 1994. Justia.com. Web. 1 March 2010.

Chrisman, Rodney D. "*Stoneridge v. Scientific-Atlanta*: Do Section 10(B) and Rule 10B-5 Require a Misstatement or Omission?" *QLR* 26.4 (2008): 839-918. Print.

Gomm, Seth S. "See No Evil, Hear No Evil, Speak No Evil: *Stoneridge Investment Partners, LLC v. Scientific-Atlanta, Inc.* and the Supreme Court's Attempt to Determine the Issue of Scheme Liability." *Arkansas Law Review* 61.3 (2009): 453-486. Print.

In re Parmalat Sec. Litig. __F. Supp. 2d__. U.S. Dist. LEXIS 6329. U.S. Dist. Ct. for the Second Circuit. 2009. LexisNexis. Web. 1 March 2010.

Prentice, Robert A. "*Stoneridge*, Securities Fraud Litigation, and the Supreme Court." *American Business Law Journal* 45.4 (2008): 611-683.

Private Securities Litigation Reform Act. Pub. L. 104-67. 04 Jan. 1995. 109 Stat. 737. Cornell Legal Information Institute. Web. 1 March 2010. Available at: <http://www.law.cornell.edu/uscode/15/usc_sec_15_00000078--u004-.html>.

Regents of the University of California v. Credit Suisse First Boston (USA), Inc. 482

F. 3d 372. U.S. Dist. Ct. for the Fifth

Circuit. 2007. LexisNexis. Web.

1 March 2010.

Rose, Amanda M. "Reforming Securities Litigation

Reform: Restructuring the Relationship

Between Public and Private Enforcement of

Rule 10B-5." *Columbia Law Review* 108.6

(2008): 1301-1364. JSTOR. Web. 1 March 2010.

Sarbanes-Oxley Act. Pub L. 107-204. 30 Jul 2002.

116 Stat.745. GPOAccess.gov. Web. 1 March

2010. Available at: <http://frwebgate.

access.gpo. gov/cgi-bin/getdoc.cgi?

dbname=107_cong_ bills&docid=f:h3763enr.

tst.pdf>

Securities Exchange Act. Pub. L. 48. 6 June 1934.

48 Stat. 881. 19 Feb. 2009. Securities

Lawyer's Deskbook. University of Cincinnati

College of Law. Web. 1 March 2010. Available

at: <http://www.law.uc.edu/CCL/34Act/>.

Simpson v. AOL Time Warner Inc. 452 F.3d 1040.

U.S. Ct. of Appeals for the Ninth Circuit.

2006. LexisNexis. Web. 1 March 2010.

Souza, Travis S. "Freedom to Defraud: *Stoneridge*,

Primary Liability, and the Need to Properly

Define Section 10(B)." *Duke Law Journal* 57.4

(2008): 1179-1207. Print.

Stoneridge Inv. Partners. LLC. v. Scientific-

Atlanta, Inc. 552 U.S. ___ . 128 S. Ct. 761.

U.S. Supreme Ct. 2008. Justia.com. Web. 1

March 2010.

## Cover Letter

Here is Kennedy's cover letter that he sent to editors of scholarly journals.

Kennedy Andrews
PO Box 0000
Chapel Hill, NC 27514
kenn.andrews@uncch.edu
(555) 555-5555

January 1, 2000

Katie Rose Guest Pryal, Editor
Minerva Undergraduate Review
PO Box 0000
Durham, NC 27701

Dear Prof. Pryal:

Please consider the enclosed manuscript "'Unequal Laws unto a Savage Race': The Validity of Student Judicial Evidence in Criminal and Civil Courts" (3,445 words) for publication in an upcoming issue of the *Minerva Undergraduate Review*. I am a senior at the University of North Carolina at Chapel Hill majoring in history and Italian; my research interests focus on the intersection of student judicial proceedings and civil and criminal trials. This article has never been considered for publication.

The *Minerva Undergraduate Review* is the perfect place to publish "'Unequal Laws'" as it directly addresses the issues of student judicial proceedings and their intersection with criminal and civil law. This work represents the culmination of my four years in a student-run judicial system as both counsel defending students and as a Deputy Student Attorney General charging students with a violation under the Honor Code. No other article addresses the interaction between evidence collected in student judicial proceedings and the evidentiary rules of civil and criminal courts. This piece provides a close reading of FERPA (Family Educational Rights and Privacy Act), a confusing federal law; furthermore it applies it to a subject largely untouched by criminal and civil courts.

Attached please find the full article plus a short abstract, in Microsoft Word format. I employed MLA citation style. I welcome any and all suggestions for revisions that the editorial board may suggest. Please feel free to contact me via email or phone; my contact information is in the letterhead. I thank you for your consideration and await your decision.

Sincerely,

Kennedy Andrews

# Works Cited

Aristotle. *Rhetoric*. Trans. W. Rhys Roberts. Mineola, NY: Dover Publications, 2004.

*The Bluebook: A Uniform System of Citation*. 18th Ed. Cambridge, MA: The Harvard Law Review Association, 2005.

Bouchoux, Deborah E. *Aspen Handbook for Legal Writers: A Practical Reference*. New York: Aspen, 2005.

Clinton, William Jefferson. "Memorandum on Plain Language in Government Writing." June 1, 1998. In *Administration of William J. Clinton, 1998*. Government Printing Office Federal Digital System. Available at: http://www.gpo.gov/fdsys/pkg/WCPD-1998-06-08/pdf/WCPD-1998-06-08-Pg1010.pdf.

Davis, Richard A. "Anatomy of a Smear Campaign." Boston.com: *The Boston Globe* online. March 21, 2004. Available at: http://www.boston.com/news/politics/president/articles/2004/03/21/ the_anatomy_of_a_smear_campaign/?page=2.

Dernbach, John C. et al. *A Practical Guide to Legal Writing and Legal Method*. 3rd Ed. New York: Aspen Publishers, 2007.

District of Columbia v. Heller. 554 U.S. ____. 128 S. Ct. 2783. Supreme Court of the United States. 2008.

Kempin, Jr., Frederick G. *Historical Introduction to Anglo-American Law in a Nutshell*. 2nd Ed. St. Paul, MN: West Publishing Co., 1973.

Jefferson, Thomas. The Declaration of Independence. 1776. Available at: http://en.wikisource.org/wiki/United_States_Declaration_of_Independence.

Lawrence v. Texas. 539 U.S. 558. Supreme Court of the United States. 2003.

McKinney, Ruth Ann. *Reading Like a Lawyer: Time-Saving Strategies for Reading Law Like an Expert*. Durham, NC: Carolina Academic Press, 2005.

Modern Language Association. *MLA Style Manual and Guide to Scholarly Publishing*. 3rd Ed. New York: Modern Language Association, 2008.

Truth, Sojourner. "Ain't I a Woman." 1851. Available at: http://en.wikisource.org/wiki/Ain%27t_I_a_Woman%3F.

Volokh, Eugene. *Academic Legal Writing: Law Reviews, Student Notes, and Seminar Papers*. New York: Foundation Press, 2003.

# Index